New
Progress
to First Certificate

Workbook with answers

Leo Jones

CAMBRIDGE
UNIVERSITY PRESS

PUBLISHED BY THE PRESS SYNDICATE OF THE UNIVERSITY OF CAMBRIDGE
The Pitt Building, Trumpington Street, Cambridge, United Kingdom

CAMBRIDGE UNIVERSITY PRESS
The Edinburgh Building, Cambridge CB2 2RU, UK
40 West 20th Street, New York, NY 10011–4211, USA
10 Stamford Road, Oakleigh, VIC 3166, Australia
Ruiz de Alarcón 13, 28014 Madrid, Spain
Dock House, The Waterfront, Cape Town 8001, South Africa

http://www.cambridge.org

© Cambridge University Press 2000   .

First published 2000
Reprinted 2001

Printed in the United Kingdom at the University Press, Cambridge

ISBN 0 521 77426 8 Workbook
ISBN 0 521 77425 X Workbook with answers
ISBN 0 521 77424 1 Workbook Cassette
ISBN 0 521 79764 0 Workbook Self-study Book
ISBN 0 521 49985 2 Student's Book
ISBN 0 521 49988 7 Self-study Student's Book
ISBN 0 521 49986 0 Teacher's Book
ISBN 0 521 49987 9 Class Cassette Set

Contents

Welcome!

This Workbook will help you to do well in the Cambridge First Certificate Exam.

Each Workbook unit contains follow-up exercises for the equivalent Student's Book unit in *New Progress to First Certificate*. (There is no Unit 20 because by then you should spend your time revising all the units in the Student's Book and the Workbook – and do FCE Exam Practice tests.)

All the exercises in this Workbook are relevant to the exam, so even if you aren't using the *New Progress to First Certificate* Student's Book, you'll find them useful as you prepare for the exam.

Do the exercises at your own speed – spend longer on the ones you find difficult and less time on the ones that are easy for you.

Each Workbook unit contains 6–8 separate exercises related to the topic and language points introduced in the Student's Book.

VOCABULARY	Revise the topic vocabulary for each unit by doing these enjoyable crosswords and word search puzzles.
READING	Develop your reading skills by reading these interesting passages. The tasks and questions help you become familiar with the tasks and questions you'll have to answer in **Paper 1: Reading**.
GRAMMAR REVIEW	Give yourself extra practice in the grammar points introduced in the Student's Book. The exercises help you to become familiar with the kind of questions you'll be asked in **Paper 3: Use of English**. You should also study the GRAMMAR REFERENCE section in the Student's Book.
WORD STUDY	Do these exercises to improve your vocabulary for all five papers of the exam, including **Part 5** of **Paper 3**.
LISTENING	Listen to the recordings and improve your listening comprehension. These exercises prepare you for the different tasks you'll have to do in **Paper 4: Listening**.
PRONUNCIATION	Use the recording to improve your pronunciation, and learn to speak more fluently so that you can do well in **Paper 5: Speaking**.
SPEAKING	Practise talking English and doing the same kind of tasks you'll have to do with a partner in **Paper 5: Speaking**. If possible, do these exercises with another student – but if that isn't possible, you can do them on your own.
WRITING	Do these writing tasks so that you can do well in **Paper 2: Writing**. The tasks are similar to the tasks you'll have to do in **Part 1** and **Part 2** of the Writing paper. When you've done each Writing task, compare your work with the Model composition.
MODEL COMPOSITIONS	Read these and see what kind of written work the examiners are hoping to see in **Paper 2: Writing**. But don't worry if your work isn't as good – you can still get a good grade if you make mistakes!
EXAM TECHNIQUES	Starting in Unit 9, as the exam gets nearer, there are special exercises to help you with the techniques you need for each paper in the exam.
EXAM TIPS	All through the Workbook, in the left-hand margin, there are tips on how to prepare and how to do well in the exam.

I'm sure this Workbook will help you to do your best in the exam.
I hope you enjoy using it!

1 Communication

1.1 Talking about language — VOCABULARY

All the words in this puzzle come in Unit 1 in the Student's Book. If you haven't already done 1.1 in the Student's Book, do this puzzle later.

Solve the clues on the left and write the words in the spaces in the puzzle on the right.

1 *Truth* is an … noun.
2 When speaking English, good … is important.
3 *Badly* and *well* are … .
4 *Communication* has five … .
5 Words in a dictionary are listed … .
6 The text on page 12 in the Student's Book is about good … .
7 Australians and New Zealanders speak English with similar … .
8 If you come across a new word you want to remember, … it in yellow.
9 *-ness* at the end of *happiness* is a … .
10 Words like *French* and *Greek* begin with a … letter.
11 People in Mediterranean and Latin countries use more … than people in Britain.
12 Re- in rewrite is a … .
13 (down) A person's … … can tell you a lot about how they feel.

1.2 Cutting noise pollution — READING

In this exercise, the ends of some sentences are missing – look for clues in the sentence structure and the content of the article. In Part 3 of the Reading paper (Paper 1) in the FCE exam you'll have to read a text from which 7 or 8 full sentences have been removed.

With this kind of exercise it's best to fill the easy gaps first and then come back to the more difficult ones later.

Six sentence endings have been removed from the article opposite. Choose from the endings (A–G) the ones which fit in each gap (1–6). There is one extra ending which you don't need to use. The first gap is already filled for you, as an example.

A after the United States.

B it is difficult to enforce such rules.

C it is ideal for putting an end to mobile-phone conversations on trains.

D jamming devices are very expensive.

E mobile jamming devices.

F provided it did not block signals for legitimate mobile-phone users nearby.

G the devices have proved extremely popular.

Jamming devices cut noise pollution among Japan's chattering classes

Jonathan Watts in Tokyo

FOR those who don't like sharing their sushi, concerts or train journeys with people having heated discussions on their mobile phones, Japanese manufacturers have come up with the latest defence – **1** *E*

With cellular chit-chat becoming more of a public nuisance every day, the government has proposed using jamming equipment to ensure that theatre and concert audiences are not interrupted by bleeps, electronic melodies and noisily hushed hellos.

Demand for the devices has come hard on the heels of a rapid growth in the market for mobile phones in Japan, which now has the second-highest number of users in the world, **2**

Among the companies cashing in on the desire for a little peace and quiet is Nikkodo, which supplies jamming equipment to hospitals and coffee shops. According to the company, **3**

On a smaller scale, SIC, a Tokyo-based manufacturer, has produced a jamming device aimed at individual customers, which sells for £276. With a range of just 3 metres, **4**

But regulators are concerned that such equipment could be misused. Last month they proposed a licensing system for the devices and said that usage should be restricted to areas where mobile phones could create significant public disturbance, **5**

Mobile phone subscriptions in Japan have soared from 300,000 in 1994 to almost 90 million today, or one in three of the population. This is largely thanks to deregulation, which has pushed prices down almost to the level of ordinary phones, and technical innovation, which has created the lightweight, powerful handsets now given free to new subscribers.

But noise pollution has become a major nuisance, prompting bans in many restaurants, cinemas, and offices.

Without technical intervention, however, **6**

Tokyo's largest railway company, JR East, has introduced a campaign to dissuade commuters from using mobile phones on trains. But few people switch their handsets off before boarding, and a single ring is usually enough to send at least three people fumbling inside their pockets or bags.

"Help!"

1.3 Word-building, synonyms and opposites

Part 5 of the Use of English paper (Paper 3) in the FCE exam tests word-building. This includes using prefixes (*un* + *natural* = *unnatural*), suffixes (*care* + *ful* = *careful*), forming compound words (*air* + *port* = *airport*) and correct spelling (*strong · strength*).

Besides preparing you for Part 5 the WORD STUDY sections in the Student's Book will also help you to improve your spelling and general vocabulary.

Sometimes it's easy to build new words from shorter words, sometimes it's harder. Write down your answers to these questions. If you don't know the answer, look the word up in an English–English dictionary.

Prefixes

What is the opposite of *comfortable*?   un*comfortable*......

What is the opposite of *possible*?   i.................................

Suffixes

What is the noun of *possible*?   p.................................

What is the adjective from the noun *power*?   p.................................

Compound words

We talk about *snowflakes, hailstones* and ...   r.................................

I take aspirin if I have a ...   h.................................

Spelling changes

What is the noun from the adjective *wide*?   w.................................

What is the adjective of the noun *pride*?   p.................................

Synonyms

Another word for *marvellous* is ...   f.................................

Another word for very *interesting* is ...   f.................................

Opposites

The opposite of *easy* is ...   d.................................

The opposite of *safe* is ...   d.................................

1.4 Present tenses

Look at pages 182–3 in the Student's Book for more examples and rules for using Present tenses.

Fill the gaps in these sentences with suitable forms of the verbs from the list below.

boil   drink   go   have   look like   speak   study   talk ✓   try   want

1 They ...*are always talking*... when they should be studying.
2 Although they are sisters, Mary and Sue .... each other.
3 Sometimes I .... coffee for breakfast but usually I just .... tea.
4 Water .... at 100° Celsius.
5 Americans and British people .... with different accents.
6 I can't go out now because I ....
7 She .... to dance classes because she .... to become a dancer.
8 Please don't interrupt me, I .... to concentrate.

Fill the gaps in these sentences with a suitable form of the verb in bold.

1 Where ...*do you come*.................................. from?   **come**
2 Why .... so sad lately?   **look**
3 They .... engaged since last October.   **be**
4 A new car .... thousands of pounds.   **cost**
5 You're late! We .... for half an hour.   **wait**
6 Which one of you .... all the milk?   **drink**
7 Next weekend I .... on a trip to the seaside.   **go**
8 .... coffee or tea?   **prefer**

1.5 Vowel sounds   PRONUNCIATION

A 🔊 Say the highlighted words and then read the full sentence aloud. Then listen to the model version and say the sentence again.

The examples are spoken in RP (Received Pronunciation = an educated southern English accent). In other accents some of these vowel sounds are pronounced differently. This exercise practises the pronunciation of vowel sounds which you will do in Unit 7.7.

sound	example	sentence
ɪ	gr**i**n	*Th**i**s sentence **is** pr**i**nted **in** **i**tal**i**cs.*
iː	gr**ee**n	W**e** don't a**gr**ee that the m**ea**nings of pr**e**fixes are **ea**sy to learn.
e	g**e**sture	**E**very dictionary contains d**e**finitions and **e**xamples and corr**e**ct sp**e**llings.
æ	h**a**ppily	H**a**rry and **A**nnie have been h**a**ppily m**a**rried since J**a**nuary.
ɑː	h**ea**rt	The c**a**stle is surrounded by a m**a**rvellous p**a**rk full of p**a**lm trees.
ɒ	sp**o**t	Will you pr**o**mise n**o**t to c**ou**gh during the c**o**ncert?
ɔː	sp**or**t	There's no w**ar**m w**a**ter on the f**or**ty-f**our**th fl**oor**.
ʊ	f**oo**t	She t**oo**k a quick l**oo**k at the b**oo**k and p**u**t it back on the shelf.
uː	sh**oe**	I'm not in a s**ui**table m**oo**d for hot f**oo**d, can I just ch**oo**se some fr**ui**t?
ʌ	h**u**ngry	It'll be f**u**n to have l**u**nch in the s**u**n when our work's d**o**ne!
ɜː	f**ir**st	'The **ear**ly bird catches the w**or**m' means 'It's w**or**th doing things **ear**ly'.

B Say these groups of words aloud – first slowly, then more quickly.

grin · green	did · deed · dead · Dad	pit · Pete · pet · pat · pot · port
lend · land	shot · short · shut · shirt	mean · men · man · moon
shut · shirt	Sid · seed · said · sad	pill · peel · Paul · pull · pool · pearl
collar · colour	fill · feel · fell · full · fool	knit · neat · net · not · nought · nut

Which sounds do you find most difficult to say? Practise these some more before you do the next exercise.

1.6 Free phone calls – with commercials   LISTENING

🔊 Listen to a broadcast about three schemes to offer free telephone calls in Sweden, the USA and in Britain. Answer the questions by writing *S* for *Sweden*, *U* for *USA*, or *B* for *Britain* in the boxes. (One or more boxes may need two letters in them.)

If you don't understand much the first time you listen, play the recording again and use the Pause control more often. Don't look at the transcript until you've played the recording through at least twice. Remember that in real life (and in the exam) there is no transcript of what people say to you – nor is there a Pause button!

1 The scheme is called FreeWay.   [ ] 1

2 You listen to a commercial before you are connected.   [ ] 2

3 Each commercial lasts 5 to 15 seconds.   [ ] 3

4 For each commercial you listen to, you get credit for a two-minute long-distance call.   [ ] 4

5 Calls are interrupted by a commercial every three minutes.   [ ] 5

6 Calls are interrupted by a commercial every two minutes.   [ ] 6

7 Callers have to dial two numbers to make a call.   [ ] 7

8 Callers have to remember their PIN number to access the service.   [ ] 8

1.7 **Mobile phones** SPEAKING AND WRITING

If possible, arrange to do **A** and **B** with another student. If this isn't possible, record your answers to the questions using a cassette recorder and a microphone. Then listen to the recording and try to improve your answers.

A Look at the two photos and make notes on your answers to these questions, using the phrases in the speech balloon below. Explain your reasons as well as giving your opinions.

1 Which person is more like you? Why?
2 When is a mobile phone most useful? Why?
3 When is a normal phone most useful? Why?
4 What do you like about using a mobile phone? Why?
5 What do you dislike about mobile phones? Why?
6 Where should mobile phones be switched off? Why?
7 Where is it OK for them to be switched on? Why?
8 Is it OK for motorists to use a mobile phone while driving? Why not?

> During the Speaking paper (Paper 5), short answers to questions are easiest of course. But longer answers are more impressive – and will get you better marks in the exam. Try to get into the habit of explaining your reasons, rather than just stating your opinion.

OPINIONS
It seems to me that . . .
I don't really think that . . .
I think it's true to say that . . .
The point is that . . .

REASONS
I feel this way because . . .
I believe so because . . .
The reason why I think so is because . . .

B Working with another student, look at the photos and ask each other the questions. Make sure you say more than just a few words in answer to each question.

or Working alone, record your answers to the questions using a cassette recorder and a microphone. Then listen to the recording and try to improve your answers.

or Speaking quietly to yourself, give your answers to each of the questions.

C Write a composition (120–180 words) giving your opinions on mobile phones beginning with these words:

I love mobile phones because . . .
or
I hate mobile phones because . . .

Count the number of words you've written. Then compare your composition with the Model composition on page 101.

> In Part 2 of the Writing paper (Paper 2) in the exam you'll have to write a composition of 120–180 words. Try to get into the habit of writing about 150 words each time you do a writing task like this.

At your service!

2.1 Shops and stores   VOCABULARY

There are 25 words connected with shopping hidden in this puzzle, including types of shops and things you can find in a shop or buy there. Circle each one you can find.

```
c h e q u e x g o o d s
p e n y l z q u e u e h
c r e d i t c a r d m o
w a w e f i y r z m a p
z s s p t l c a w y r h
f s a a w l o n x v k a
a i g r y b u t c h e r
s s e t z w n e a y t m
h t n m v a t e s z w a
i a t e a y e w h t x c
o n v n b a r g a i n y
n t z t s w e a t e r z
```

2.2 Questions and question tags   GRAMMAR REVIEW

A

Questions are mostly used in conversations of course, aren't they? But do you realise that they can be useful in writing too? In writing, what can you do before you explain something? You can ask a question.

Rewrite each of these questions beginning with the words below.

1 What time is it?   Do you happen to know ...what..time..it..is........... ?

2 Are you going shopping on Saturday?   Could you tell me .... ?

3 When does the supermarket open?   Can you tell me .... ?

4 Where are the toilets?   Do you know .... ?

5 Where did you buy those blue shoes?   May I ask .... ?

6 How much does a pair of shoes like   I'd like to know ....
   that cost?

7 Who did you go to town with?   Please tell me ....

8 How much money have you spent?   Do you know how .... ?

B

Why are questions useful in writing? Questions catch the reader's attention and make the writing seem more personal. For example: "What do I hate most about shopping? Well, first of all …"

Write the correct question tag at the end of each sentence.

1 You've bought some new shoes, ...haven't you... ?

2 Post offices in the UK are closed on Sundays, ... ?

3 Most banks open on Saturday mornings, ... ?

4 We can change money at a *bureau de change,* .... ?

5 If you want to buy something at a kiosk you can't use a credit card, ... ?

6 Let's not worry about it, ... ?

7 There didn't seem to be many people in town this afternoon, ... ?

8 You forgot to buy me a sandwich, ... ?

2.3 Levis jeans

READING

Seven paragraphs have been removed from this article. Choose from paragraphs A–G the ones which fit in each gap (1–7). The first gap is already filled for you as an example.

A But in 1853 he went to San Francisco, then booming after the Gold Rush, and set up his own dry goods company. When he died in 1902 his nephews inherited a thriving business dealing in dry goods and making Levi jeans.

B But it was some time in 1873, the year Levi Strauss and Jacob Davis patented the idea, that would ultimately make Levi jeans world famous.

C Careful market research boosted European sales of Levi's by 80%. The twin messages were "these are the original jeans" and "don't they look sexy".

D Davis suggested they jointly apply for the patent and manufacture the strengthened "waist overalls". Strauss saw the potential, signed up and the two went into business.

E Strauss first bought his material from an east coast textile mill which had also made arms during the American civil war. His company was later to switch to a mill in North Carolina, the centre of denim production in the US.

F The back-to-basics policy worked. The flagship 501s are essentially the same as the jeans sold to miners, cowboys and farmhands in the 1800s.

G The company and the Levi Strauss Foundation last year made charitable donations totalling $20m to bodies involved in causes such as the fight against Aids, racism and discrimination.

Brand values: Levis

No one knows exactly when the first pair of Levi jeans was made. All records were lost when the Levi Strauss head office was destroyed by fire during the 1906 San Francisco earthquake.

1 B

Davis, a Latvian-born tailor working in Reno, Nevada, came up with the idea of inserting copper rivets into trousers to give them extra strength, after one of his customers complained of pockets ripping. Davis could not afford the $68 needed to patent his idea, so he turned to the man from whom he bought his cloth, Levi Strauss, who ran a wholesale dry goods business in San Francisco.

2

Levi Strauss & Co's first jeans had one back pocket, riveted in the corners, a watch pocket, and buttons for braces. The two back pockets so familiar on today's jeans did not appear until 1902. In 1937 the rivets were covered with cloth in response to customer complaints that they scratched furniture and saddles. The red tab was introduced in 1936 to help salesmen identify Levi jeans at rodeos.

3

Strauss was born Loeb Strauss in Buttenheim, Bavaria, in 1829 and emigrated to the United States where he worked in his brothers' dry goods business in New York and changed his first name to Levi.

4

Levi Strauss & Co, which pulled out of wholesaling in 1948, is still a family-owned firm today. The company's carefully cultivated image of a socially caring business was damaged earlier this year when it announced the closure of 11 US factories, the loss of 5,900 jobs, and a search for cheaper production facilities overseas. It is a far cry from the founder's decision in 1887 to fund 28 scholarships at the University of California. Scholarships are still available today.

5

Remarkably for what is now a global icon symbolising the casual, unpretentious American way of life, Levi jeans only started to be sold throughout the US in the 1950s. Overseas sales coincided with the rise of youth culture of the 1960s.

6

But in a disastrous move in the 1970s, the company tried to sell products from baby clothing to polyester suits under the Levi brand and soon started to lose money. Since then it has introduced non-jeans lines under different brand names. The company then realised the importance of brand perception. It was its status as the original blue jeans maker that enabled it to charge premium prices.

7

A few years ago teenagers would have given their eyeteeth for a pair. Now designer labels and cargo pants are flavour of the moment. But denim will rise again.

2.4 Abbreviations and numbers   WORD STUDY

A

Write these abbreviations out in full.

1 Xmas   *Christmas*

2 Feb.   ....

3 Wed.   ....

4 info.   ....

5 approx.   ....

6 UK   ....

7 Sq.   ....

8 40 W. 20th St. ....

Most people find numbers *very* hard to say in a foreign language. And hard to understand too. Say numbers aloud slowly and clearly in English.

B

Write the answers to these arithmetic questions out in full.

1 $707 + 70$ = *seven hundred and seventy-seven*

2 22.2×2 = ...

3 $1{,}111 + 123$ = ...

4 $17 \div 2$ = ...

5 $3\frac{1}{2} + 4\frac{1}{4}$ = ...

6 $56 \div 4$ = ...

7 $1{,}000 - 222$ = ...

8 3×10^{6} = ...

And don't be afraid to say: 'I'm sorry, could you say that number again, please?' if you want someone to repeat a number.

2.5 Can I help you?   LISTENING

▣ **Listen to people talking in five different situations. Choose the best answer (A, B or C) for each question.**

In Part I of the Listening paper (Paper 4) you'll have to do a test quite like this one. To answer the questions you don't need to understand everything – just look at the questions and listen carefully for the relevant information.

1 Two people are talking. What are they talking about?
   A a pair of trousers   **B** a skirt   **C** a dress   **1**

2 Two people are in a bank. How much commission will the bank charge the customer?
   A 2 per cent   **B** 5 euros   **C** 5 dollars   **2**

3 Two people are in a pharmacy (chemist's). What does the man buy?
   A lozenges   **B** syrup   **C** inhaler   **3**

4 Two people are in a post office. How does the woman send the package to her nephew?
   A by surface mail   **B** by normal airmail   **C** as airmail printed papers   **4**

5 Two people are in a market. How much does the woman save?
   A £5.50   **B** £3.00   **C** £2.00   **5**

2.6 / **Agreeing and disagreeing**   SPEAKING

If possible, arrange to do this exercise with another student. If this isn't possible, record your answers to the questions using a cassette recorder and a microphone. Then listen to the recording and try to improve your answers.

A Here are some people's opinions. Make notes on what you'd say in response to them, using the phrases in the speech balloons below. If you disagree, explain your reasons for disagreeing.

1 'Shops should all be open 24 hours a day, 7 days a week.'
2 'The commercials on TV are usually more entertaining than the programmes.'
3 'There's no point in buying expensive clothes. It's a waste of money.'
4 'Clothes in bright colours like red and yellow are becoming fashionable.'
5 'People spend too much money buying things they don't really need.'
6 'Everything is cheaper in a supermarket than in a street market.'

> That's true. And I also think that . . .
> I agree with you. And I also think that . . .
> That's a good point. Don't you also think that . . . ?
> I see what you mean, but . . .

> Well, personally, I think that . . .
> I don't really agree because . . .
> I don't quite agree because . . .
> That's an interesting point of view, but I think . . .

In Part 4 of the Speaking paper (Paper 5) you'll take part in a three-way discussion with another candidate and an examiner. If you disagree with either of them, it's important to sound friendly and polite – not aggressive or rude.

B Working with another student, take turns to respond to each opinion. Make sure you say more than just a few words in response.

or Working alone, record your answers to the questions using a cassette recorder and a microphone. Then listen to the recording and try to improve your responses.

or Speaking quietly to yourself, say your responses to each of the opinions.

"Can I call you back? I'm shopping"

2.7 Please send me a refund . . . WRITING

A Imagine that you bought a pair of designer jeans by mail order. You weren't satisfied with your purchase. Look at the catalogue information and your notes.

In real life, if you write a business letter, you should include your own address, the name and address of the reader and today's date. In the exam you shouldn't include any of these.

Designer warehouse

Offering you the latest name in high quality designer gear at cost prices direct from the manufacturer! Choose from:

Top brand jeans complete with rivet pockets and side seam details, prices start at £19.99

Sport logo tops in the latest fabric, prices from £9.99

Designer label trainers in this summer's colours, from £24.99

Buy one pair of jeans and get a pair of trainers half price.

Do it now before the summer has gone!

All of this and more from: Jeans Direct

- side seam tore first time I wore them
- no rivet on back pockets
- zip broke
- invoice showed that I was charged £29.99 — more expensive than in ad and than I can buy in the shops
- returning: 1 pair of jeans
- full refund please

B Write a letter (120–180 words) to the Customer Relations Manager of the mail-order company, complaining about their product. Include all the relevant information from the catalogue and your notes. Begin like this:

In Part I of the Writing paper (Paper 2) you'll have to write a letter, based on information and notes that you have to read. The style you use (friendly/informal or formal) must be appropriate to the situation.

> Dear Sir or Madam,
>
> Last week I received from you...

and end like this:

> Please send me a full refund of £29.99.
> Thank you,
> Yours faithfully,

C Count the number of words you've written. Then compare your composition with the Model composition on page 101.

3 Friends and relations

VOCABULARY

Add the missing words to the puzzle on the right.

1 Let's all go out for a meal on your … .
2 My parents have been … for 25 years.
3 Mary is Sally's aunt, so Sally is Mary's … .
4 John and Mary have two sons and one … .
5 My grandfather's sister is my … - … .
6 Ann and Bill are getting married in June. Bill is her …
7 and Ann is Bill's … .
8 The date of the … is June 15th.
9 Ann is Sally's … friend.
10 Another word for *relations* is … .
11 Next month is my parents' 25th wedding … .
12 Tony and Sue split up last year and now they are … .
13 Mary is Tony's aunt, so Tony is Mary's … .
14 Derek is Tony's father's father, so Tony is Derek's … .
15 The party after a wedding is called the … .
16 My sister's husband is my … - … - … .
17 They fell in … at first sight.
18 Most children call their mother '…'.
19 (down) The most important people at a wedding are the … … … .

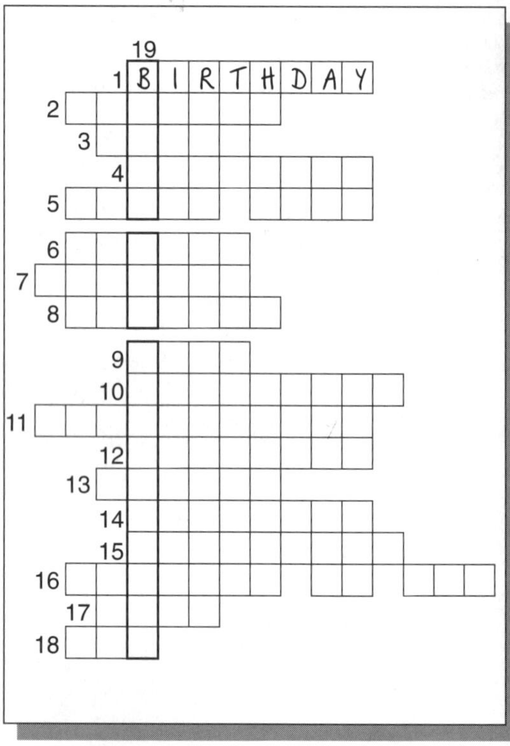

(crossword grid with 1 across: BIRTHDAY, 19 down: B)

3.2 Here comes the bride! READING

Read this newspaper article and then answer the questions on the next page. Choose the answer A, B or C, which you think is best according to the text.

Here comes the bride, whoever she is

By MAURICE WEAVER

THE bride, a model, wore a dress of ivory fabric and the groom, an ex-miner, a look of understandable distraction yesterday as Britain's first blind-date wedding went ahead despite the disapproval of the Church.

The defining moment at the marriage of Gregory Cordell and Carla Germaine came when, minutes after they first met, he was asked what he thought of the stranger who was now his wife. After a pause, he stammered: "I couldn't have made a better choice myself."

Gregory, 27, and Carla, 23, had done without the romance of finding each other by chance and missed the sweet dance of courtship and engagement. Theirs was a marriage made in media-land.

Everything from first match-making to compatibility assessment, hire of dress to booking of honeymoon was done for them by the staff of BRMB, their local pop radio station in Birmingham. The catch phrase was: "Love on the airwaves."

They were the lucky ones out of 100 men and 110 women, mostly 20-somethings, who applied for the "roles" when they were advertised last November. Psychologists, counsellors and even an astrologer did the rest, much of it on the air.

Radio executives, having spent £50,000 on the project, stood proudly by in the Concerto Room of Birmingham's Hyatt Hotel as the handsome pair made their vows in return for a Bahamas holiday and a free flat and car for a year. The station was not allowed to broadcast the ceremony live, so the couple's vows to "love, trust, honour and care" had to be recorded for broadcasting later.

When Carla threw back her veil it was the first time Greg had set eyes on her. He looked very grand in his rented wedding suit and tie. Not surprisingly he got his words mixed up with nervousness and she actually seemed to choke back a tear.

They added their own lines to the ceremony, promising to "strive to love" for the rest of their lives. It went: "I commit myself to you and to our future life. I shall stand by you as lover and friend whatever may come. I shall be honest in sharing your hopes and fears …"

Then they exchanged gold rings, each with the station's call-sign BRMB 96.4FM inscribed inside to show who was paying the bills. In the hotel outside the marriage room were lots of balloons with BRMB logos in case anyone forgot.

Greg, a former coal-miner who became a television security salesman, was born and bred in Tamworth and enjoys rugby and kick-boxing.

Carla, from Sutton Coldfield, West Midlands, has blonde good looks that keep her in local modelling and advertising work. She says her mother, Maureen, was uneasy about her unusual marriage plans at first but eventually gave in, and her father, Graham, turned up to give her away. Before the ceremony Mrs Germaine shrugged philosophically and said: "She's a level-headed girl. She'll cope."

To prove that it was "happy families" all round, the bride's younger sister and two friends were bridesmaids, while Greg's father, his step-mother and his three brothers turned up too. They were entertained to a fancy wedding breakfast … courtesy of BRMB, of course.

Carla, looking far more relaxed than her groom, said she was "extremely pleased" at the way things had turned out. The bride said she was delighted with her husband. Gazing at Greg and sounding rather like a mail-order shopper assessing what the postman had brought, she said: "I told them from Day One what I liked and he is very, very good."

She knew that the Church, not to mention some of her friends, thought her irresponsible. "But this is what I chose to do," she said. "I am my own person. There was no pressure. Everyone is entitled to their own views, aren't they?"

Greg thought his bride was "stunning". As for the marriage's chances, he could only say that he planned to "put 100 per cent behind it".

BRMB's spokesman, Michael Owen, insisted that the project was "a serious experiment". When asked how he justified that, he replied: "The Church has said marriage is a God-given thing but I think there is an argument that perhaps it isn't any more. After all, don't they predict that only 40 per cent of couples will be married next century? Perhaps people should be more objective about it. We hope they will react, feel involved and form their own opinions on what we have done."

Of course, he admitted, the station hoped it would attract more listeners. The Church's intervention had "raised the whole profile" of the promotion by adding to the controversy. Mr Owen said that if Greg and Carla had problems, of whatever kind, BRMB would be ready with counsellors to try to save the radio station's investment.

Last night the new Mr and Mrs Cordell entertained 100 friends at a wedding party and then retired to the Hyatt Hotel's £750-a-night Chamberlain Suite for their wedding night. ∎

In Part 2 of the Reading paper (Paper 1) you'll have to read a newspaper or magazine article or a story and answer 7 or 8 multiple-choice questions. In the exam there are four possible answers to each question: A, B, C or D.

1 According to the article, who arranged for the wedding?
A Gregory   B Carla   C BRMB

2 How many people entered the competition that Gregory and Carla won?
A 20   B 110   C 210

3 How were listeners able to listen to the wedding ceremony?
A Live   B They heard a recording.   C They couldn't hear it because it wasn't broadcast.

4 When did Greg first see Carla's face?
A in a photograph   B before the ceremony   C during the ceremony

5 What is Carla's job?
A She's a broadcaster.   B She's a model.   C She's unemployed.

6 How many of their relations attended the wedding ceremony?
A 8   B 5   C 10

7 What were their first impressions of each other?
A disappointment   B satisfaction   C delight

8 If the marriage runs into trouble what will the radio station do to help?
A ask the Church for advice   B provide counselling   C nothing

3.3 **Using prefixes – 1**   WORD STUDY

A Look at the examples and fill the gaps.

re	= again	heated up again: *reheated*	arrange again: ....
pre-	= before	already cooked: *pre-cooked*	before the exam: ....
post-	= after	after the war: *post-war*	after lunch: ....
over-	= too much	cooked for too long: *overcooked*	very crowded: ....
under	= not enough	not cooked enough: *undercooked*	not prepared enough: ....

B Use the words in bold at the end of each line to form new words to fit in the spaces.

1 After his wife died he never ....   **marry**

2 I asked for my steak rare but this steak is ....   **do**

3 We .... the number of people who would come – only five turned up.   **estimate**

4 Leningrad was .... St Petersburg in 1991.   **name**

5 The oven must be .... before you put the food in to cook.   **heat**

6 I think you're wrong. Will you please .... your decision?   **consider**

7 We thought she'd gone for ever, but she .... in the spring.   **appear**

8 £4.99 for a birthday card? That seems extraordinarily .... !   **price**

3.4 **The past – 1**   GRAMMAR REVIEW

A Write the past and past participles of these verbs in the gaps.

If you still make mistakes with past and past participle forms of irregular verbs, you should spend some time revising them. Look at page 108.

speak	*spoke*	*spoken*	forget	....	....
write	....	....	take	....	....
stick	....	....	hear	....	....
drive	....	....	try	....	....
run	....	....	break	....	....

B Fill each gap in this news story with a suitable verb from the list below.

In Part 1 and Part 2 of the Use of English paper you'll have to read a story and fill the gaps. Part 1 consists of 15 gaps and you have a choice of four possible words to fill each gap. Part 2 also has 15 gaps but you have to fill each gap with any suitable word you can think of.

An Australian couple who [1] *agreed* to a blind-date wedding in September last year did not live happily ever after. They [2]................... at the altar, after Leif Bunyan, 22, who [3]................... herself as the "typical, clean-living, all-action Australian girl", [4]................... a competition organised by a Sydney radio station. She was selected from more than 300 women with Glenn Emerton and $40,000 of extras were offered as first prize. They never even [5]................... a photograph of each other and they [6]................... once when he [7]................... on air.

However, two months later, they [8]................... . The bride [9]................... that her 24-year-old husband's bond with his identical twin brother was one of the major problems.

Mr Emerton was initially delighted with his new bride. He [10]...................: "She was interrogated by my best friends, subjected to a lie detector test and various psychological profiles. How could she not be my perfect partner?" The couple [11]................... their honeymoon in Paris, but the trip [12]................... to spark any romance.

agree ✔   describe   enter   explain   fail   spend   meet
propose   say   see   separate   speak

3.5 Diphthongs · PRONUNCIATION

A Say the highlighted words and then read the full sentence aloud. Then listen to the model version and say the sentence again.

You probably find some of these sounds easier to say than others. Have another try at saying the ones you found more difficult before you do the next exercise.

sound	example	sentence
eɪ	plane	The <u>rain</u> in <u>Spain</u> stays <u>mainly</u> on the <u>plain</u>.
aɪ	eye	<u>Clive</u> <u>tried</u> to <u>find</u> a <u>white</u> <u>bicycle</u> on <u>Friday</u>.
ɔɪ	boy	That <u>annoying</u> <u>boy</u> has a <u>noisy</u> <u>voice</u> and he's <u>spoiling</u> my <u>enjoyment</u>.
aʊ	mouth	The <u>crowd</u> marched <u>around</u> the <u>town</u> <u>shouting</u> <u>loudly</u>.
əʊ	nose	<u>Only</u> <u>Joe</u> <u>knows</u> that <u>Joan</u> <u>spoke</u> to <u>Tony</u> on the <u>phone</u> at <u>home</u>.
ɪə	hear	<u>Dear</u> old Mr <u>Fielding</u> <u>clearly</u> has <u>years</u> and <u>years</u> of <u>experience</u>.
eə	hair	<u>Mary</u> <u>repaired</u> the <u>chair</u> and carried it <u>carefully</u> up the <u>stairs</u>.

B Say these groups of words aloud – first slowly, then more quickly.

pain · pine	male · mile · mole · mill · meal	her · who · Hey! · Hi! · how · hear · hair
town · tone	lick · lack · lock · luck · lake · like	see · say · sigh · so
hair · here	pay · pie · pier · pair	sick · suck · sock · sake · soak
hate · height	find · found · phoned	fair · fur · four · far

Which sounds do you find most difficult to say? Practise these some more before you do the next exercise.

3.6 A sad romance · LISTENING

In Part 4 of the Listening paper (Paper 4) you'll have to listen to part of a broadcast or conversation and decide if statements are true or false, or decide which of the speakers mentioned particular points.

Captain Corelli's Mandolin by Louis de Bernières is a best-selling novel. Its story takes place on the Greek island of Cephalonia, and is about a love affair between an Italian officer and a Greek woman during World War II.

 Listen to the story of a sad love affair. Decide which of the following statements are TRUE and which are FALSE. Write T or F in the boxes.

1 Luigi Surace and Angeliki Stratigou met during World War II. ☐ 1

2 They fell in love and got engaged. ☐ 2

3 Angeliki's aunt liked Luigi. ☐ 3

4 Angeliki, who still lived in Patras, remained unmarried all her life. ☐ 4

5 Luigi forgot all about Angeliki. ☐ 5

6 Luigi tried to find Angeliki after his wife had died. ☐ 6

7 Nancy Pavlopoulou helped them to get back together. ☐ 7

3.7 Telling and writing a story

SPEAKING AND WRITING

If possible, arrange to do **A** and **B** with another student. If this isn't possible, record your answers to the questions using a cassette recorder and a microphone. Then listen to the recording and try to improve your answers.

1

2

A Look at the two illustrations. Imagine that you are one of the two friends in the scenes, which happened on the same day. Make notes on your answers to these questions, using the phrases in the speech balloon below.

If you include some dialogue in a story, it helps to make it seem more lively and realistic. But make sure your punctuation is correct.

1 How did the day begin?
2 What happened just before the first scene?
3 What happened in the first scene? What did you say to each other?
4 What happened between the first and second scenes?
5 What happened in the second scene? What did you say to each other?
6 What happened just after the second scene?
7 What happened in the end? How did the day end?

B Working with another student, ask each other the questions. Make sure you say more than just a few words in answer to each question.

Even when you're writing a story about something that happened to you, making notes is a good idea. In the exam you shouldn't write more than 180 words, and this can be difficult if you get involved in a long story.

or Working alone, record your answers to the questions using a cassette recorder and a microphone. Then listen to the recording and try to improve your answers.

or Speaking quietly to yourself, give your answers to each of the questions.

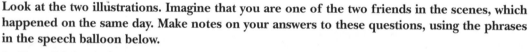

It all began when . . .
I said to my friend, "Why . . . ?"
We were so surprised when . . .
After that we . . .

The next thing that happened was . . .
My friend asked me, "When . . . ?"
We were really relieved when . . .
And in the end we . . .

C Write the story (120–180 words) of what happened to you on that day, beginning or ending with these words:

You can only write a very short story in 120–180 words!

What a day!

Count the number of words you've written. Then compare your composition with the Model composition on page 101.

Time off

4.1 Sports and leisure activities   VOCABULARY

There are 24 sports, hobbies and games hidden in this puzzle.
Circle each one you can find. (Some words may be hidden in other words.)

```
z  x  d  f  b  w  a  c  a  r  d  s  w
s  d  a  w  a  r  e  m  u  s  i  c  a
w  i  n  d  s  u  r  f  i  n  g  y  t
i  v  c  z  k  n  o  o  r  q  x  c  e
m  i  i  b  e  n  b  o  e  h  t  l  r
m  n  n  a  t  i  i  t  a  c  e  i  s
i  g  g  d  b  n  c  b  d  h  n  n  k
n  k  o  m  a  g  s  a  i  e  n  g  i
g  a  l  i  l  e  r  l  n  s  i  y  i
p  r  f  n  l  o  o  l  g  s  s  o  n
p  h  o  t  o  g  r  a  p  h  y  g  g
m  c  o  o  k  e  r  y  o  g  a  t  e
p  a  i  n  t  i  n  g  d  a  r  t  s
```

If you speak in a polite, friendly tone of voice, people will react pleasantly to you. Also, reacting pleasantly to what others say is important.

4.2 A friendly, polite tone of voice   PRONUNCIATION

If you have something negative or unpleasant to say, hesitating helps to make you sound friendly, rather than critical or aggressive.

 A

Nodding, keeping eye contact and smiling at the other person who is speaking is good, and so are phrases like "I see", "Absolutely" and "That's interesting!".

 Say these sentences aloud in a polite and friendly tone – imagine that you're having a discussion with someone you don't know very well. Then listen to the model versions and say the sentences again.

1 I'm sorry to interrupt, but ...er... could I just say something?
2 I'm sorry, but I ...er... I don't really agree.
3 Well, I see what you mean, but ...er... I don't think that's right.
4 Don't you think you're ...er... exaggerating a little?
5 Well, I think you're being a little ...er... extreme.
6 I don't think what you said ...er... really makes sense.

B

Hesitating is also a useful way to gain time when speaking:
"Well, . . ."
"Let me see, . . ."
"Let me think, . . ."
"Well, actually, . . ."
"Um . . ."

Decide where you can insert *Well* or *...er...* or *...um...* into these sentences to make them sound less negative and unpleasant. Say the sentences aloud. Then listen to the model versions on the cassette and try to imitate the tone of voice.

1 I'm sorry, but I think you're being a bit silly.
2 No, you're wrong about that, I think.
3 I'm afraid I don't really agree with you.
4 I think you're wrong about that.
5 I've been waiting for you. You're rather late.
6 I'm afraid I've got some bad news for you.

Cheese Races, 1998

Look at this newspaper article and choose the most suitable summary sentence from the list A–H for each paragraph (1–7) in the article. There's one extra summary sentence which you don't need to use.

In Part 1 of the Reading paper (Paper 1) you may have to do a task like this (with a longer text) or a similar task where you have to choose suitable headings for each paragraph.

A 25 people chased the cheese down the hill.

B Four participants ran down the hill.

C It is stupid to talk about safety at an event like this.

D Luckily no participants were hurt this year.

E One cheese rolled down the hill. ✔

F The race was banned because two safety teams were not available.

G The race was held in secret because the authorities cancelled the public races.

H We didn't want to cancel the event but we were forced to.

Secret Cheese Race at Dawn

by Ben Fenton

1 [E]

A SOLITARY cheese of liberty rolled down Cooper's Hill at dawn yesterday, rescuing a centuries-old tradition from the threat of bureaucratic suffocation.

2

The event, which local people say predates the Norman Conquest, was banned by Gloucestershire county council, which owns the hill. So, in the first light of the bank holiday, a group of about 25 dedicated cheese enthusiasts crept on to the slope and, after a short opening ceremony, four champions of individual freedom hurtled downwards in pursuit of the rolling cheese.

3

All four reached the bottom without injury, an outcome which was unusual for the race, which last year saw 13 of the 30 or so competitors injured over four races. The 1996 toll was even higher.

4

Tony Peasley, a member of the cheese-rolling committee said: "We did it to maintain the continuity of the cheese-rolling tradition. There were the normal formalities and then just one cheese was rolled down the hill. There were just four racers who went after it and everyone escaped unscathed. It was a great success."

5

The winner was Peter Astman, a local postman, and the ladies' winner was Amelia Hardwick. Yesterday Mr Peasley said: "I would just like to say sorry to all the people who have raced in other years, but who were not able to be there this time. Hopefully by next year all the troubles will have been resolved and it will go ahead as normal." This year's attempt to run the cheeses on the hill near Gloucester was abandoned because the absence of the cave rescue team at the top of the slope led the St John's Ambulance team at the bottom to refuse to act alone.

6

Mr Peasley said at the time: "The county council asked us if we had consulted with the Health and Safety Executive. But if you start talking about the Health and Safety Executive at a cheese-rolling event, you start to wonder where it will all end. Gloucestershire county council has completely washed its hands of this.

7

"We had no choice other than to cancel this year's official event. It was very sad to have to do so but our hands were tied. The council wanted us to show them insurance certificates to avoid receiving injury claims because the hill is on their land."

4.4 The past – 2   GRAMMAR REVIEW

Read this article about the 1999 cheese-rolling race and fill the gaps with suitable forms of the verbs on the right.

You may need to use

the past:	*won* *was/were winning*
or the present perfect:	*has/have gone* *has/have been going*
or the past perfect:	*had gone* *had been going*
or the passive:	*was/were won* *has/have been won* *had been won*

In Part 1 of the Use of English paper (Paper 3) you have a choice of four possible words to fit in each gap. Do the easy ones first, then come back to the ones you couldn't do first time through.

Builder becomes champion cheese racer

A BUILDER ¹ ..went.. went home with three giant Double Gloucester cheeses yesterday after a triple triumph in one of Britain's oldest Bank Holiday traditions despite safety fears.   **go**

Steve Brain, 30, ² .... all three men's races in the historic Cooper's Hill cheese-rolling competition, which ³ .... 2,000 spectators. Mr Brain, a rugby player from Matson, ⁴ .... rivals hurling themselves down the dangerous 45 degree slope in pursuit of the 3.5 kilo cheeses.   **win** **attract** **beat**

Mr Brain ⁵ .... regularly .... in the races since he was 15.
He ⁶ .... 13 of the specially-made cheeses before this year's hat trick.   **take part** **win**

He said: "The secret of winning is to stay on your feet as much as possible."

The women's race attracted two competitors and ⁷ .... by Helen Thorp, 19, of Brockworth. Her friend, Sabrina Rimmer, 18, ⁸ .... second.   **win** **come**

Races ⁹ .... for hundreds of years on the Cotswold slope.
But they ¹⁰ .... last year because of safety fears after 33 people ¹¹ .... , seven of them spectators hit by a cheese, in 1997. Cheeses bounce and can reach speeds of up to 60 kph.   **hold** **cancel** **injure**

Gloucestershire County Council ¹² .... for extra safety measures before the event could resume. Organisers brought in 15 professional marshals and ¹³ .... extra fencing to help protect spectactors. Six people ¹⁴ .... slightly .... yesterday, but ¹⁵ .... not .... to hospital.   **call** **install** **hurt** **take**

4.5 Using prefixes – 2   WORD STUDY

Use the words at the end of each line to form new words to fit in the spaces.

1 The audience in the theatre are seated in a ..semi–circle.. around the stage.   **circle**

2 He's older than 30, I'd say he was in his ....   **thirty**

3 Ugh! Someone has left a .... sandwich on my desk.   **eat**

4 She stopped in .... because she had to sneeze.   **sentence**

5 He works best on his own, he's very ....   **motivate**

6 The door was .... so we both went inside.   **open**

7 Some matches are played at the weekend and others are played ....   **week**

8 A pessimist would say a bottle is ....   **empty**

   – an optimist would say it's ....   **full**

4.6 Swimming with sharks

LISTENING

 Listen to a broadcast about Ben Lecomte's record-breaking swim across the Atlantic. Fill in the missing information in the notes.

1 How long did the swim take?

`_____` **1**

2 Number of hours per day he was in the water:

`_____` **2**

3 Where did he sleep? `_____` **3**

4 How fast did he swim? `_____` **4**

5 Furthest distance he swam in a day: `_____` **5**

6 Ben's nationality: `_____` **6**

7 He did the swim to raise money for: `_____` **7**

8 On August 20 Ben felt an `_____` **8**

9 How far off his route were the Azores? `_____` **9**

10 Number of days he spent ashore in the Azores: `_____` **10**

11 How close did a shark come to him? `_____` **11**

12 His first words as he waded ashore at Port Maria: `_____` **12**

4.7 Dangerous sports

SPEAKING

If possible, arrange to do this exercise with another student. If this isn't possible, record your answers to the questions using a cassette recorder and a microphone. Then listen to the recording and try to improve your answers.

A Make notes on your answers to these questions, using the phrases in the speech balloon below.

1 Would you like to take part in the cheese race (see 4.3 and 4.4)? Why/Why not?
2 Would you like to watch the race? Why/Why not?
3 What do you think about Ben Lecomte's achievement (see above)?
4 What do you think drives a person like Ben to swim, row or sail across the ocean?
5 What is the longest you've ever swum, walked or ridden? How did you feel afterwards?
6 Do you sometimes take risks, or do you try to avoid danger?

> It seems to me that . . .
> I can understand why . . . but I can't understand why . . .
> I really admire people who . . .
>
> People who do this kind of thing are . . .
> It puzzles me that some people . . .
> I can't imagine anything I'd hate more than . . .

B Working with another student, ask each other the questions. Make sure you say more than just a few words in answer to each question.

or Working alone, record your answers to the questions using a cassette recorder and a microphone. Then listen to the recording and try to improve your answers.

or Speaking quietly to yourself, give your answers to each of the questions.

4.8 Dear Ms Green . . .   WRITING

A

Imagine that you are organising a fun run to raise money for charity. You have just received this letter from a local department store. Read the letter and your notes carefully.

In Part 1 of the Writing paper (Paper 2) you may have to answer a letter (as here), or read some information, notes or an advertisement and then write a letter or write for further information – whatever it is make sure you read the information very carefully and include all the relevant information in your letter. You'll lose marks if you don't include all the major points.

Thank you for your letter about the Fun Run you are organising. We also support the charity.

Several members of our staff are keen runners and would certainly like to take part. Several other less fit members might also like to take part if the run isn't too strenuous!

Before we all commit ourselves, however, there are a few questions I'd like to ask you:

- What distance is the course?

The course is fairly level but there is one steep hill up and then down.

Circular: 2 km or 4 km twice round.

- Have you organised first aid facilities? If not, we would be pleased to do this for you. Our firm has its own first aid team.

Yes, please!

- Would you like us to donate a t-shirt to every participant? We have in mind something with the name of the charity on it and our own logo (very small).

No, I've already arranged T-shirts.

- Will there be prizes for the fastest runners?

No, it's a fun run, not a race.

- Have you organised refreshments for runners during and after the run?

No, would you be able to do this instead of T-shirts?

We look forward to hearing from you.

Yours truly,

SM Green

Susan Green

P.S. Please send us 50 sponsorship forms.

Two enclosed – please photocopy as many as you like.

B

Now write a reply to Ms Green giving the information requested and also covering the notes you have written (120–180 words).

This kind of letter needs to be written in an appropriate style. Here not too familiar and not too formal is probably OK. So, not like you'd write to a good friend – and also not the kind of style you might use if you were applying for a job.

Here are some phrases you can use in your letter:

Dear Ms Green,

Thank you for your interest in . . .

In answer to your questions: . . .

It is very generous of you to offer to . . .

Thank you also for offering to . . .

I'm afraid that there will not . . .

Again, thank you for writing to me.

I can assure you that . . .

I am delighted to accept your offer.

I am sorry to tell you that I have already . . .

Would you by any chance be willing to . . . ?

I enclose two . . .

C

Count the number of words you've written. Then compare your composition with the Model composition on page 102.

5 The world around us

Nature and the weather

VOCABULARY

Add the words to the puzzle on the right.

1 A small amount of rain.
2 Lots of trees together.
3 A very high wind.
4 Something that grows in the ground.
5 What you see before you hear thunder.
6 A place where it doesn't rain.
7 This is measured in degrees Celsius.
8 It's quite difficult to see in this type of weather.
9 These are the most intelligent of all animals.
10 You only get this when it's below zero.
11 A light wind.
12 You can't see the sun if the weather is like this.
13 A whale is this kind of animal.
14 A wasp is this kind of creature.
15 A period of very hot weather.
16 (down) Watch this to find out what it's going to be like tomorrow.

5.2 The ice-storm

READING

Seven clauses have been removed from the article opposite. Choose from the clauses (A–H) the ones which fit in each gap (1–7). There is one extra clause which you don't need to use. The first gap is already filled for you, as an example.

Some of the words are printed in bold type. These are words which refer back to ideas previously mentioned. They are 'clues' which can help you to decide which sentences fit into blanks 1–7.

Always read the sentences through first. Then read the article. Then fit in the easy ones and number them to remind you where they go. Then come back to the harder ones later.

Look for clues in the text: words like *it* (referring back to a thing or idea mentioned earlier), *he* (referring back to a person mentioned earlier), *this* (referring back to an action or idea mentioned earlier), etc.

A **they** expected to be there for some time

B **it** fell for days, and **it** paralysed much of Quebec

C most could expect to wait at least a week before **it** was restored

D Mr Bouchard had urged **them** to stay shut until Thursday

E the temperature fell sharply after **that**

F **the troops** have had to be given police powers

G four of the five transmission systems that supply **the city** and its 2 million-plus people were still out

H **they** have even slipped under snow-dumpers

(The capital letters at the start of a new sentence have been removed to make the task harder!)

Canada. After the storm, the clearing-up

IT WAS the worst ice-storm in living memory. What started in the clouds as rain became ice as it hit power lines, trees and roads. **1** 8 knocking out the power supply to 3m people – nearly half the province's inhabitants – and hundreds of thousands more in New Brunswick, to the south, and westward in eastern Ontario. Well over 100,000 people had to escape from their freezing homes to those of luckier or better-equipped neighbours or for shelter in public buildings. Quebec's premier, Lucien Bouchard, even appealed to the federal government to send in troops. The damage amounts to at least C$2 billion ($1.4 billion). And the clearing-up is still far from complete.

The collapse of pylons and cables under the weight of ice cut off power to Montreal. At midweek, **2** . In West Montreal, where power had been restored, over-demand on Monday plunged homes and offices back into darkness and cold. Most schools, universities, and government offices were closed because **3** , to prevent an overload that could knock out the system again. Power was to be rationed for a week; full repair will take longer.

Life this week was worse than that in outlying suburbs and an area south of the city, now known as "the triangle of darkness", where hundreds of thousands of households – indeed some whole towns – still lacked light, heat and water. In some towns most of the people had been evacuated to temporary shelters, usually schools heated by generators. **4** – and glad of it: the midweek forecast was for more ferocious weather, with temperatures that might fall to minus 50 degrees. In all, at midweek well over 1m people were without power. **5** .

The affected area was in chaos. Some 600 huge electricity pylons had crumpled under the weight of ice like giant toys; at least 30,000 wooden poles lay on the snow-covered ground like matchsticks. In towns, broken power lines, covered in ice, trailed across streets, many of these still blocked by trees brought down by the weight of ice. The known death toll is not large, but rising: people have been crushed by ice falling from roofs, electrocuted by fallen power-lines; **6** . Others trying to heat their homes with portable barbecues have poisoned themselves; at least nine have died.

Meanwhile, police and troops have been going from door to door persuading people to move out of still blacked-out homes, worried at the risk of extreme cold, especially to old people, as temperatures fall. And there are other, less deadly, risks than the cold, unfortunately. **7** to protect evacuated areas from looting. Faced with shared disaster, would the Canadians of pre-electric centuries have needed to be restrained from such nastiness?

5.3 Using prefixes – 3 WORD STUDY

A Write the negative forms of these adjectives.

kind ...unkind................   possible ....   patient ....

legible ....   relevant ....   appropriate ....

efficient ....   fortunate ....

clear ....   mature ....

formal ....   accurate ....

B Use the words at the end of each line to form new words to fit in the spaces.

In Part 5 of the Use of English paper (Paper 3), you may have to add a prefix and a suffix to the root words given (e.g. un + will + ing = unwilling).

1 If your signature is ...illegible................ it's hard for anyone to copy it. **legible**

2 I think I .... you: did you really ask for honey in your coffee? **hear**

3 .... I really can't help you. **fortune**

4 You'll lose marks in the exam for grammatical .... **accurate**

5 'All trains will be delayed. We apologise for the ....' **convenient**

6 She was .... to go out with him at such short notice. **will**

7 I'm afraid I will be .... to help you with your work. **able**

8 The children were punished for .... their parents. **obey**

5.4 Articles and quantifiers – 1 GRAMMAR REVIEW

A Fill each gap in these phrases with a suitable word.

a ...loaf/slice... of bread   a .... of water   a .... of milk

a .... of coffee   a .... of beer   a .... of chocolate

a .... of information   a .... of wine   a .... of news

B Complete the second sentence so that it has a similar meaning to the first sentence, using the word on the left. Use between two and five words, including the word given. Don't change the word given.

See also Articles and quantifiers on pages 171–172 in the Student's Book.

1 Can you advise me how to remember vocabulary?

advice Could you ...give me some advice on.... remembering vocabulary?

2 There was a huge amount of rain and the streets were flooded.

rained It .... the streets were flooded.

3 There were so many cars that we couldn't get across the road.

traffic There .... it was impossible to cross the road.

4 How large was the concert audience?

attended How .... the concert?

5 They had fewer suitcases and bags than I expected them to have.

luggage They didn't .... I expected.

6 We'd like a room for tonight.

accommodation Do .... available for tonight?

7 Education is compulsory up to the age of 16.

school Children have to .... until they're 16.

8 Rain is forecast for today.

weather According to the forecast .... today.

Consonants   **PRONUNCIATION**

A Say the examples aloud. Listen to the model versions on the cassette. Then say the words again.

In the Speaking paper (Paper 5) you will be marked on your pronunciation, but you aren't expected to speak English with a perfect British accent. Your own national accent of English is fine, provided that people can understand you easily.

sounds	examples		
p · b	path · bath	Paul · ball	rope · robe
t · d	seat · seed	two · do	town · down
k · g	cold · gold	Kate · gate	docks · dogs
f · v	few · view	off · of	leaf · leave
s · z	niece · knees	ice · eyes	Sue · zoo
r · l	arrive · alive	fright · flight	grass · glass
ʃ · s	she · see	shoe · Sue	shock · sock
s · θ	sick · thick	sing · thing	mouse · mouth
z · ð	breeze · breathe	close (*verb*) · clothe	
ts · tʃ	cats · catch	beats · beach	Ritz · rich
ʃ · tʃ	shoes · choose	share · chair	shop · chop
h · –	hand · and	hate · eight	heat · eat
v · w	vest · west	vine · wine	verse · worse
j · dʒ	yet · jet	your · jaw	use (*noun*) · juice
ʒ · z	pleasure	vision	confusion

B Read each of these 'tongue twisters' aloud – first slowly, then more quickly.

Native speakers also find these tongue twisters difficult!

p · b	Bees were buzzing in the bushes beside the path in the public park.
t · d	David's Dad wanted to be seated beside David at the wedding reception.
k · g	Gordon got Kate a cardigan because she felt cold in the garden.
f · v	The view of the fields across the valley from the farm was fabulous.
s · z	Sue goes to the zoo to see the zebras, lions and tigers every summer.
r · l	We would like to welcome you to our airline and wish you a pleasant flight.
ʃ · s	Sally shouldn't share her soup and sandwiches with Sam, should she?
s · θ	Three hundred and thirty-three Swiss soldiers started to sing songs together.
z · ð	The brothers have won more prizes than their cousins.
tʃ · ts	Charles is rich but he sits in the cheap seats at football matches.
ʃ · tʃ	Charlie's English pronunciation is much better than Charlotte's.
h · –	Harry hopes that he'll have a whole hour at the art gallery before Hugh arrives.
v · w	I wonder why Will won't visit Vicky without an invitation.
j · dʒ	George tells jokes about journeys and universities, but you haven't laughed yet.
ʒ · z	As usual it was a pleasure to see you – please visit us on another occasion.

Which sounds did you find most difficult to say? Highlight the examples and sentences in **A** and **B** which you found hard to say correctly. Then practise saying them again.

In Part 3 of the Listening paper (Paper 4) you'll hear five people, each talking for a few seconds – not two talking for a whole minute, as here. The one-minute talks in this recording are similar to the one-minute talk you'll have to give in Part 2 of the Speaking paper.

| 5.6 | **One-minute talks** | LISTENING |

🔊 Listen to Angela and Bill talking about keeping animals as pets. Decide which of them gave the opinions below. Write A (Angela) or B (Bill) in the boxes.

1 Children can benefit from having a pet.

2 Dogs have to be taken for walks.

3 Dogs make a lot of noise and may scare children.

4 Large dogs need a lot of exercise.

5 If you have a dog it restricts your life.

6 It's unkind to leave a dog alone in a city apartment.

| 5.7 | **Talking for a minute: Pets** | SPEAKING AND WRITING |

If possible, arrange to do **A** and **B** with another student. If this isn't possible, record your talk using a cassette recorder and a microphone. Then listen to the recording and try to improve your talk.

In Part 2 of the Speaking paper (Paper 5) you'll have two photos to talk about for a minute. You are asked to compare and contrast them. Don't describe all the things you can see. Just talk about the *differences* between the pictures and your *reactions* to what they show.

A Prepare a one-minute talk about the photos above. Think what you can say to compare and contrast the two pictures and say how you feel about them. There's no need to describe the pictures in detail.

B Working with another student, each of you should talk for a minute about the photos. Then discuss how you could improve your talks.

or Working alone, record your one-minute talk using a cassette recorder and a microphone. Then listen to the recording and try to improve your talk.

or Speaking softly to yourself, give your one-minute talk.

C Write an article for a student magazine explaining your views on keeping animals as pets (120–180 words). Begin by making notes:

POINTS AGAINST   POINTS IN FAVOUR

Count the number of words you've written. Then compare your composition with the Model composition on page 102.

Going places

6.1 Travel and transport

VOCABULARY

There are 25 words connected
with cars, roads and transport
hidden in this puzzle.
Circle each one you can find.

b	x	c	m	o	t	o	r	w	a	y	t	f
u	p	a	v	e	m	e	n	t	y	s	r	l
s	a	q	z	f	a	r	e	d	t	e	a	i
r	t	p	e	d	e	s	t	r	i	a	n	g
o	h	a	c	a	r	t	r	i	p	t	s	h
u	b	r	a	k	e	r	s	v	e	b	p	t
n	h	k	m	e	t	r	o	i	o	e	o	c
d	u	a	c	c	i	d	e	n	t	l	r	y
a	s	p	e	e	d	i	n	g	i	t	t	c
b	f	u	e	l	a	o	u	t	i	n	g	l
o	r	f	j	o	u	r	n	e	y	s	b	i
u	c	a	u	b	y	p	a	s	s	e	k	s
t	a	x	i	j	u	n	c	t	i	o	n	t

6.2 Articles – 2

GRAMMAR REVIEW

Fill each gap in this news story with *a* or *the*. (Some of the gaps can take either *a* or *the*.)

Soaked with spring rain, [1]............... grass on these hillsides shines in [2]............... May sunshine. Streams flooded with melted snow rush towards [3]............... Missouri river. The meadowlark sings at full blast. Then comes the high-pitched noise of tyres against road as vehicles speed up in anticipation of hitting [4]............... Montana border. But the days of speeding will soon be no more. As of May 28th, Montana will have [5]............... 75mph speed limit. This, to some people's regret, has spelled [6]............... end of "Montanabahn".

In 1995, when [7]............... federal government stopped requiring every state to have [8]............... speed limit, Montana settled for [9]............... "basic rule", which merely obliged motorists to drive in "[10]............... reasonable and prudent manner" based on traffic, road and weather conditions. Only at night was [11]............... speed limit set, [12]............... sensible 65mph (105kph).

Montana natives took this new liberty in their stride. Accustomed to long drives (it is 980km from Sidney to Missoula), [13]............... locals know that [14]............... thrill of rocketing along at 115mph (185kph) is outweighed by [15]............... stiff neck and [16]............... tension headache. Visitors, however, had other ideas. In [17]............... spring of 1996, motorists noticed [18]............... convoy of 15 Mercedes-Benz cars on Highway 191 north of Yellowstone National Park. Travelling at 95mph, they were driving aggressively – hugging each other's tails and passing each other on dangerously short stretches of straight road. Worried by such behaviour on [19]............... two-lane road already known for accidents, [20]............... Montana Highway Patrol stopped them. They were German tourists, interpreting "reasonable and prudent" in their own way.

Montana's Supreme Court also found [21]............... law confusing. Last December it decided that ²² .... "basic rule" was too vague, because drivers could not be sure whether they were obeying the law. Montana re-introduced ²³ .... speed limit. Curiously, safety was not ²⁴ .... prime argument. According to Arnie Mohl, the sponsor of ²⁵ .... bill for ²⁶ .... speed limit, 'When we had the "basic rule", our accident rate went down and our death rate went down. We had accidents, but most of them were at night, when we had a speed limit.' Montana now joins ten other states, all in ²⁷ .... West, which enforce ²⁸ .... 75mph (120kph) speed limit on Interstate highways. Only one state, Hawaii, remains at 55mph.

For those keen to watch ²⁹ .... mileposts whizz by, Montana did allow one consolation. If you are caught going at up to 85mph, ³⁰ .... fine is only $20, and it doesn't go on your driving record.

6.3 Words with several syllables PRONUNCIATION

 A 📼 Say the words and then read the full sentence aloud. Then listen to the model version and say the sentence again.

words	sentence
encourage · encouragement	She didn't encourage me at all, but he gave me a lot of encouragement.
pronounce · pronunciation	How do you pronounce the word *pronunciation*?
imagine · imagination	I can't imagine what's going to happen because I haven't got a very good imagination.
prefer · preference	I prefer to go by taxi. What's your preference?
explain · explanation	I asked him to explain again because I didn't understand his explanation the first time.
popular · popularity	*Star Wars* is popular again. Its popularity never seems to get less.
accurate · accuracy	Make sure your spelling is accurate because in the exam you lose marks for inaccuracy.
generous · generosity	You have been very generous. I didn't expect such generosity.
simple · simplicity	Directions should be simple, not complicated. People appreciate simplicity.

B Say these words aloud – first slowly, then more quickly.

semi-automatic	self-respect	underprepared
overweight	uncomfortable	inexperienced
unpleasantness	inconvenient	transport
reality	efficiency	improbability

Which words do you find most difficult to say? Practise these some more before you do the next exercise.

6.4 Young drivers in California   READING

Look at this newspaper article and choose the most suitable summary sentence from the list A–F for each paragraph (1–5) in the article. There's one extra summary sentence which you don't need to use.

In Part 1 of the Reading paper (Paper 1) there are 7 missing summary sentences, plus an example. Sometimes there may be missing headings for each paragraph of the article.

A   Californian teenage drivers are angry about the new laws.

B   Elderly drivers also cause accidents.

C   Many teenagers tried to beat the 1st July deadline.

D   New laws for young drivers in California.

E   New laws were introduced in other US states.

F   Teenage drivers cause more accidents than other drivers.

Bad days for young drivers

1

SINCE July 1st, large numbers of Californian teenagers (those suntanned creatures devoted to open-top cars) have been having a hard time. The reason: all those obtaining their driving licences after that date are prohibited for a year from driving at night unless accompanied by someone over the age of 25. Worse, during the first six months of driving, they may not carry any passengers under the age of 20. They cannot get a licence at all until they have completed 50 hours of driving, ten of them at night, under adult supervision; and they cannot get a full licence until they have driven for a year with no violations.

2

All this is very much stricter than the previous regulations, as many a movie suggests; which explains why, in the days before July 1st, every local office of the California Motor Vehicle Department was crammed with desperate young people. But the state has been moved to act – as others have – by the disproportionate involvement of teenagers in fatal accidents.

3

In California, 16–19-year-olds make up 3.9% of the state's 20m motorists; but they account for 10.2% of all drivers in injury collisions and 8.9% of those in collisions that prove fatal. Across the country, 14% of all drivers involved in fatal crashes in 1996 were 15–20 years old. In the words of the CMVD, which could be echoed round the world, "inexperience, immature judgment and a tendency to take risks place teens at a disadvantage behind the wheel."

4

It was Maryland, in the mid-1970s, that first analysed accidents by age-group and, as a result, brought in tougher restrictions on young drivers. After two decades, collisions involving young drivers fell by 10%. But the state was still unhappy, and last year a new law came in that required a written diary recording all supervised practice time with an adult, as well as 18 months of driving without violations. California's new law is modelled on one introduced in 1986 in Michigan, where over 500 specially trained testers have been recruited to examine the new drivers.

5

California's teenage rebels might protest, however, that they are not the only dangerous people on the state's roads. The largest group involved in accidents between midnight and 3am are drivers in their early 20s, and this is also the largest group involved in accidents caused by alcohol. As for future trends, the number of teenage drivers is falling, while the numbers of those over 65 – many of them have poor eyesight, slow reactions and take pills – is growing fast. The most dangerous driver in California is not necessarily the James Dean lookalike in the red sports car with three girls, but the grandfather in the golf-cart who drifts out of the Senior Retirement Centre into the fast lane.

6.5 / **People on the move**   LISTENING

 Listen to people talking in five different situations. Choose the best answer (A, B or C) for each question.

1 Two people are travelling. Where are they?
   A in a bus   **B** in a taxi   **C** on a plane

   [1]

2 The man asks a woman for directions. Where does she tell him to go?
   A straight on and first left   **B** first left and straight on   **C** left and left again

   [2]

3 The woman wants a rail ticket to Newcastle. How much does she pay?
   A £15   **B** £30.50   **C** £50

   [3]

4 The man wants to take a bus. Where does he have to buy a ticket?
   A on the bus   **B** at a kiosk   **C** at the bus stop

   [4]

5 The woman wants to get to London. Which is the cheapest way to get there?
   A by coach   **B** by train   **C** by plane

   [5]

6.6 / **Public transport**   SPEAKING

If possible, arrange to do this exercise with another student. If this isn't possible, record your answers to the questions using a cassette recorder and a microphone. Then listen to the recording and try to improve your answers.

A

Make notes on what you'd say in response to these questions. Explain your reasons as well as giving your opinions.

1 What do you think of the public transport system in your town or city?
   How could it be improved?

2 When do you use public transport – and when do you go by car?

3 When do you go by bike?
   When do you walk more than a few hundred metres?

4 When would you go somewhere by taxi?

5 How long does it take to get from your home to the centre?
   Why does it take so long?

6 What is the traffic like in your area?
   What could the local government do to improve traffic flow?

> Try to avoid giving very short answers to questions like the ones in 6.6A.

B

Working with another student, take turns to answer each question. Make sure you say more than just a few words in response.

or   **Working alone, record your answers to the questions using a cassette recorder and a microphone. Then listen to the recording and try to improve your responses.**

or   **Speaking quietly to yourself, give your answers to each of the questions.**

> In the exam it's best to answer every question with a couple of sentences, not just a couple of words.

6.7 / What do you recommend?   WRITING

Your friend Bob has written this letter to you. You have phoned two recommended companies and made notes on their prices and other information.

Read the letter, the information about the companies and your notes carefully.

In Part 1 of the Writing paper (Paper 2), always read the instructions very carefully to make sure you know exactly what is required. In Bob's letter, look at the underlined phrase: do you think he would like the information on the limo?

> After the wedding, we want to spend Saturday and Sunday driving around having a look at the country. We don't need accommodation because we can spend Saturday night back at Mary's parents' house. We don't mind sharing the driving. There are four of us who are qualified drivers and over 25. But maybe a bus with a driver would be better, even if it's a little bit more expensive.
>
> Can you find out about some local mini-bus firms and how much they would charge for two full days, self-drive or with a driver.
>
> Please just let me know what the best two options are – I don't need to know all the details.
>
> There are eight of us altogether – plus you if you'd like to join us.
>
> Best wishes,
>
> Bob

Costs shared between 8 or 9 people!

N.B.

Yes please, if I'm free that weekend.

EXCELSIOR

Self-drive minibuses for hire

* ★ 8 seats
* ★ 12 seats
* ★ 17 seats

* ◗ unlimited mileage
* ◗ special weekend rates
* ◗ drivers must be over 21

£99 – small for 8 adults (and no room for me).
£140 – plenty of room to stretch out.
£150 – very large but difficult to drive?

PULLMAN

Chauffeur-driven cars, minibuses and limos

* • 14-seater minibus
* • 10-seater luxury executive minibus
* • Super-stretch American limousine (up to 10 seats)

* ◗ *Mobile phones in all cars*
* ◗ *Experienced drivers*
* ◗ *Professional service*

More relaxing than self-drive.

£299 – plenty of room inside, but seats quite hard.
£310 – very comfortable seats and big windows.
£350 – looks great but probably not practical.

They'd know the area well.

 Write a letter to Bob, giving your recommendations (120–180 words).

C Count the number of words you've written. Then compare your composition with the Model composition on page 102.

7 There's no place like home

At home   VOCABULARY

Add the missing words to the puzzle on the right.

1 Another word for *flat*.
2 Walls can be covered with this.
3 Where the cooking is done.
4 We're going to … to another flat.
5 A woman who rents you a room.
6 You can sit in the open air on this, if your flat has one.
7 You put things in this piece of furniture.
8 These are the outer, residential parts of a city.
9 Draw these at night to stop people seeing you.
10 A chest of … .
11 This is a storage room underground.
12 I put the book back on the top … .
13 This is a grassy area where you can sit.
14 A little old house in the country.
15 If you have a garden, you might keep your lawnmower in this.
16 You hang clothes in this piece of furniture.
17 This is an underground room.
18 You have to pay this to your landlord.
19 (down) Say this to welcome someone who's visiting you at home. (4 words)

Crossword: 1 APARTMENT (19 down starts at M)

7.2 **Paris bus drivers in London**   READING

In Part 2 of the Reading paper (Paper 1) there are 7 or 8 multiple-choice questions, each with 4 possible answers to choose between.

Read this article about Paris bus drivers working in London. For Questions 1–6, choose the answer (A, B or C) which you think fits best according to the text.

1 How many French bus drivers do London United want to employ altogether?
   A 103   B 94   C 53

2 What did Jeromie Pons find most difficult?
   A speaking to the passengers   B finding his way around London
   C understanding where passengers wanted to go

3 Why does Jean-Gustave Pinchon find it hard to understand people?
   A No-one speaks with an accent he understands.   B People talk too fast.
   C Most people speak with an accent that's difficult to understand.

4 What's different about the way French drivers drive?
   A They aren't used to roundabouts.   B They drive too quickly.
   C They forget to drive on the left.

5 Why is London General employing French drivers?
   A There is more unemployment in France than London.
   B They are part of a French company.
   C French drivers are better than British ones.

6 What does Mr Pons do when a customer is angry?
   A He ignores them.   B He stays calm and apologises.   C He shouts back.

Parisians take wheel on London buses

Amelia Gentleman

A TOUCH of Parisian glamour has been added to a number of London's bus routes. In an effort to resolve a serious recruitment problem, London United, one of the country's largest bus companies, has appointed 53 French bus drivers.

Eight of the drivers are navigating their way through London, and the other 45 are in training. The company is advertising in northern France for another 50.

But the innovative employment strategy has not been without teething problems. Jeromie Pons, 24, from Paris, was one of the first recruits.

From the cab of a 94 bus in the Shepherd's Bush depot yesterday he said linguistic difficulties had proved very difficult. "I didn't understand anything, especially the way people said the names of places. I had to tell them to ask the other passengers, or ask them for help myself."

Mr Pons, whose familiarity with London geography was not very good at first, said his standard reply to inquiries like "Does this bus go to Hammersmith?" was a not very reassuring "probably".

Jean-Gustave Pinchon, 35, also from Paris, agreed language was the main problem. "There aren't many people who speak proper BBC English, so often it's very hard to understand them."

The latest batch of recruits has been given a week-long intensive English course, and their supervisors bravely insist things are going pretty well.

Reg Robinson, one of the driving instructors, said the first thing each French recruit had to learn was to slow down. "There is a tendency for them to drive much faster. Of course things don't always go smoothly, especially with the language. You might say to a guy, 'I want you to turn left at the round-about', and then watch him turn right. But if they haven't driven in this country before, we give them a few days' extra training to make sure they're happy with driving on the left."

British colleagues have been welcoming. Paul Habard, depot manager, was impressed by the quality of recruits. "Being a bus driver in France is a much more prestigious job than it is here. They don't let any old person drive a bus there; they take the cream, so that's what we're getting."

London United is a subsidiary of Transdev, one of the biggest public transport companies in France, which is why they decided to advertise there when recruitment here became difficult.

Ray Lorraine, spokesman for London United, said: "There is a shortage of bus drivers all over London, particularly in south-west and west London, where there's high employment. We've had a huge response to the adverts we put out in France, where unemployment is higher."

Mr Pons said he has had to acquire some British coolness to cope with working in London. "When I started at the company, every time a passenger came to me for an argument I would get involved and shout back. That's a very French characteristic, very Latin. Now I just say sorry and smile.

"I've also begun to understand British sarcasm. At the end of a bumpy ride passengers sometimes say 'Thank you, driver, for that very smooth journey'. To begin with I thought this was very strange."

The French drivers are organising a boules league and planning a Bastille Day party for July 14, but most are still coming to terms with bus depot canteen food. Mr Pinchon said: "The tea is very good, but the food – it is impossible to take pleasure in it."

7.3 Spelling and pronunciation – 1: Vowels WORD STUDY

One or two words in each sentence are misspelt. <u>Underline</u> the incorrect spellings and write the correct spellings at the end of the line.

1 *I liked the pasta with tomato <u>source</u> but I couldn't decide <u>weather</u> the tomatoes were fresh.*   ...*sauce*...*whether*...

2 *Which root does this bus take? Does it go via Hammersmith?*   ....

3 *She past the exam with flying colours.*   ....

4 *Could you please cheque my answers? I'm not shore if they're correct.*   ....

5 *He lent his bike against the wall but forgot too lock it.*   ....

6 *They said they new witch way to go, but they still got lost.*   ....

7 *He was feeling quite week because he had the flew.*   ....

8 *I like your shoes, have you warn them before?*   ....

7.4 Modal verbs – 1 GRAMMAR REVIEW

A

Use these verbs to fill the gaps in the sentences below.

**can/can't   could/couldn't   must/mustn't   might/mightn't
have to/don't have to   should/shouldn't   may/may not**

1 May I help you?   ...*Can*... I help you?

2 It's possible that is correct.   That .... be correct.

3 She isn't able to do it.   She .... do it.

4 Can it be true ?   .... it be true?

5 You need to show your passport.   You .... show your passport.

6 There's no need to book a table.   You .... book a table.

7 You can't park on the pavement.   You .... park on the pavement.

8 What do you advise me to do?   What .... I do?

B

Complete the second sentence so that it has a similar meaning to the first sentence, using the word in bold. Use between two and five words, including the word given. Don't change the word given.

1 Surely you're joking.
  can   You ...*can't be / cannot be*... serious.

2 You can get here after 9 o'clock if you like.
  have   You .... get here before 9 o'clock.

3 It's a good idea to walk home with someone else at night.
  alone   You .... at night.

4 I think the train will possibly be delayed.
  late   The train ....

5 I'm sure that he doesn't come from Brazil.
  be   He .... Brazilian.

6 You don't have to make notes, but it is a good idea to.
  need   Although you .... notes, I would advise you to.

7 Can we use pencils in the exam?
  allowed   Are .... in pencil in the exam?

8 You must only use a pencil for filling in lozenges on the Answer sheets.
  can   A pencil .... for filling in lozenges on the Answer sheets.

> In Part 3 of the Use of English paper (Paper 3) you have to put between two and five words in the gaps. A contracted form (*needn't*, *don't*, *haven't*) counts as two words. If you prefer to write *need not*, *do not* or *have not*, that's fine.

7.5 Saying long sentences — PRONUNCIATION

A

Say these numbers aloud.

£50m fifty million pounds   1,000 one thousand

1879 eighteen seventy-nine   2001 two thousand and one

2003 two thousand and three   4,000 four thousand

B

🔊 Listen to the complete reading of this newspaper article. Notice the way the reader's voice rises and falls in each sentence. Then REWIND the cassette.

In the Speaking paper (Paper 5) of the exam you won't have to read aloud. But reading aloud is a useful skill in real life – you may sometimes want to quote an amusing sentence from a news report or from an advertisement, for example.

Bridge link for Mont Saint-Michel

Paul Webster in Paris

tide = the rise and fall of the sea that happens twice every day
ebb = when the tide is going out
flow = when the tide is coming in
estuary = tidal part of a river
causeway = road raised above sea level

A scheme costing £50m to make Mont Saint-Michel an island again by destroying the causeway that has linked it to the mainland since 1879 was revealed yesterday.

By 2003, the causeway and the huge car park that disfigures France's most visited provincial monument, will be replaced by a bridge.

A shuttle service of little trains will carry tourists to the base of the 1,000-year-old Benedictine abbey.

The two-kilometre-long causeway has been blamed for blocking the ebb and flow of the tide into the estuary, leading to a build-up of sand dunes.

Even Atlantic high tides will be unable to reach the base of the monument within a few years.

In a report submitted to the government yesterday, scientists recommended that work start in 2001.

Once the bridge is in place the natural tidal flow should quickly sweep away deposits of sand.

The car park will be replaced by a space for about 4,000 cars about two kilometres inland.

C

🔊 Read each sentence in the article aloud. Listen to the model version of the sentence and then PAUSE the cassette. Then read the next sentence, and so on. Keep pausing the cassette.

7.6 Welcome to Heritage Park! — LISTENING

In Part 2 of the Listening paper (Paper 4) you'll have to do an exercise like this with 10 gaps to fill. Each gap requires one word or a short phrase. This is the only part of the exam where incorrect spelling doesn't lose marks!

🔊 Listen to a broadcast about a new town in South Africa, which was inspired by Mont Saint-Michel. For Questions 1–10, complete the notes which summarise what the speaker says.

Heritage Park

Heritage Park will have its own ☐ **1** of 40 men.

The new town will be surrounded by an ☐ **2**

When George Hazledon was a boy in London, you could ☐ **3**

and ☐ **4** on your own.

Heritage Park will be a community which doesn't have to ☐ **5**

Heritage Park is ☐ **6** from the sea.

George Hazledon came to South Africa ☐ **7** ago.

There are ☐ **8** people living outside the town now.

Mr Hazledon is planning to build ☐ **9** homes for them.

Eventually, there will be ☐ **10** homes in Heritage Park.

7.7   A safe place to live?   SPEAKING AND WRITING

If possible, arrange to do **A** and **B** with another student. If this isn't possible, record your answers to the questions using a cassette recorder and a microphone. Then listen to the recording and try to improve your answers.

A   **Make notes on your answers to these questions. Give your opinion and explain your reasons.**

1 How is the place you live different from Heritage Park (see above)?

2 What would it be like to live somewhere like Heritage Park?

3 Would a new suburb like Heritage Park be popular in your country? Why/Why not?

4 How much do people worry about security in the place where you live?

B   **Working with another student, ask each other the questions. Make sure you say more than just a few words in answer to each question.**

or Working alone, record your answers to the questions using a cassette recorder and a microphone. Then listen to the recording and try to improve your answers.

or Speaking quietly to yourself, give your answers to each of the questions.

C   **Write a composition (120–180 words) giving your opinions on this statement:**

> **Life is much more dangerous now than in the past.**

Count the number of words you've written. Then compare your composition with the Model composition on page 102.

If you include personal experiences in this kind of composition, the reader is more likely to be interested. But what if you don't have any relevant experiences? In the exam, you can invent them! Use your imagination!!

Looking after yourself

8.1 Good health and illness   VOCABULARY

There are 27 words connected with illness and health hidden in this puzzle. Circle each one you can find. (There are also several words *not* connected with the topic!)

a	f	i	t	v	b	r	u	i	s	e	w	b
p	l	a	y	a	d	i	s	e	a	s	e	e
i	n	j	e	c	t	i	o	n	w	i	l	d
n	i	c	e	c	o	u	g	h	m	c	l	e
f	u	n	a	i	g	o	k	s	e	k	c	c
e	a	s	y	n	p	a	i	r	d	i	e	t
c	u	r	e	e	o	l	f	a	i	n	t	i
t	a	b	l	e	t	s	s	z	c	u	t	s
i	d	q	p	a	i	n	p	p	i	l	l	n
o	r	w	a	c	h	e	o	s	n	i	f	f
n	u	r	s	e	s	e	t	f	e	v	e	r
b	g	h	u	r	t	z	h	e	a	l	t	h
l	o	t	e	m	p	e	r	a	t	u	r	e

8.2 Modal verbs – 2   GRAMMAR REVIEW

Complete the second sentence so that it has a similar meaning to the first sentence, using the word in bold. Use between two and five words, including the word given. Don't change the word given.

1 I think you probably made a mistake.

  got   You ..must have got.............. something wrong.

2 I'm sure the test was easier than you said it was.

  difficult   The test can't .... you said it was.

3 Waiting for three hours was unnecessary.

  waited   You .... for three hours.

4 No wonder you're feeling tired, you woke up too early.

  woken   You .... , then you wouldn't be feeling tired.

5 I wonder if she left a message on the answering machine.

  may   She .... a message on the answering machine.

6 Luckily, after the ship sank, they managed to swim to shore.

  swim   Luckily, they .... to shore after the ship went down.

7 Was it really necessary for you to run all the way here?

  have   .... run all the way here?

8 I stayed awake all last night.

  sleep   I .... last night.

Six sentences have been removed from the article below. Choose from the sentences (A–G) the ones which fit in each gap (1–6). There is one extra sentence which you don't need to use.

Remember to look for clues in the text. Words and phrases like *it this that he she the noise* often refer to people or ideas mentioned previously in the same paragraph. Try to spot the connections.

A As the candle burns down – the linen just turns to ash – it gets very hot, which made me slightly anxious.

B It sounds like do-it-yourself torture.

C Nevertheless, afterwards I was calm and clear, and my ears felt as though they'd had a soft little massage.

D So I settled down for some "gentle thermotherapy of the head and ears".

E That sounds like something we all need.

F The noise in my ears was terrifying.

G There is also a crackling sound, which is disconcerting.

TREATMENT OF THE WEEK:

Katharine Viner lights a Hopi ear candle

When you think of alternative therapies, you tend not to think of sticking a burning candle in your ear. **1** [8] Nevertheless, Hopi ear candles are huge on the Continent, imported from the Native American Hopi who have used them for centuries. They are said to clear ear and sinus problems, headaches, ringing in the ears and impacted wax; to activate blood and energy flow; to ease stress; and, most thrillingly, to "co-ordinate the cerebral hemispheres". **2** [ ]

3 [ ] The candles are hollow tubes of stiff linen impregnated with herbs, and I roped in a friend (who said I looked like a birthday cake) to hold them upright. The first surprise when a lit candle is inserted in your ear is the noise. It's like the whoosh inside a conch shell at the seaside and it is a lovely, relaxing sound. **4** [ ] Once I'd got used to the snap of the flame, however, I felt quite sleepy and forgot the ridiculousness of my position.

Time passed gently and I had a sensation of clarity in my normally confused head, as if my sinuses had been opened up and expanded. This is apparently an effect of what Biosun, the manufacturers, call the "medicinal herbs" which impregnate the candle – sage, camomile and St John's Wort. **5** [ ] At one point I thought that my hair might get singed, but my friend assured me the flame was still inches away.

6 [ ] I have no idea if my cerebral hemispheres were co-ordinated, but the experience was pleasant enough. One tip, though: it's disturbing if friends light cigarettes from your flame.

8.4 Spelling and pronunciation – 2: Diphthongs   WORD STUDY

Two or three words in each sentence are misspelt. <u>Underline</u> the incorrect spellings and write the correct spellings at the end of the line.

1 *I'll <u>right</u> the notes and then you can read them <u>allowed</u> to everyone.*   write aloud

2 *I didn't want to where out my new pear of shoes, so I war the old ones.*   ....

3 *Please weight for me while I read my male, then we can go out.*   ....

4 *Bred is maid with flower, yeast and water.*   ....

5 *Don't waist your money on a fir coat, even if it is in the sail.*   ....

6 *She went hire and hire up the stares until she got to the top floor.*   ....

7 *Don't by a knew car – a second-hand one is cheaper.*   ....

8 *It's not fare that we're not aloud to use dictionaries in the exam.*   ....

8.5 Intonation: Reading aloud   PRONUNCIATION

🔊 First listen to the recording once or twice. Notice how the reader's voice rises and falls in each paragraph. Then read the article aloud. Then listen to the recording again.

or If you prefer, you could pause the cassette after each paragraph, and then read the paragraph yourself, trying to use the same intonation.

Headache? Don't take a pill!

MOST people take a painkiller if they have a headache, but according to the Pain Research Institute, relaxation may be a better treatment. Tension headaches are the most common type of headache and are not usually caused by anxiety, but by muscle tension in the neck.

Here are three pill-free ways of getting relief from a headache:

1 Breathing
Sit with your back straight for 20 minutes, rest your hands on your lap and loosen your shoulders. Breathe in deeply through your nose, hold your breath for a few seconds and then breathe out slowly. Repeat this ten times.

2 Relax your muscles
Spend about 30 minutes tensing each muscle group in your body, one by one. Feel the effect and then relax. Begin with your jaw and work down to your toes, muscle by muscle.

3 Aromatherapy
Fill a small bowl of water with five drops of essential oil of rosemary and soak a flannel in it. Squeeze the flannel out and, after folding it lengthwise, lie back and gently press it to your forehead for a few seconds. Then re-soak the flannel and put it round the back of your neck and pull both ends gently.

8.6 Poetry can cure you   LISTENING

🔲 Listen to an interview with a doctor who believes that poetry can make people well. Choose the best answer, A, B or C.

1 Who did Dr Stewart read a poem called *Leisure* to?
   A all his patients **B** a business person **C** Mr Davies

   | 1

2 How did this poem help?
   A He stopped worrying. **B** He reconsidered his life.
   C He felt more relaxed.

   | 2

3 Which seems to be more effective, according to Dr Stewart?
   A listening to poetry **B** reading poetry **C** writing poetry

   | 3

4 Why do patients say that writing poetry is calming?
   A They can express their emotions. **B** The rhythm is soothing.
   C It takes a long time.

   | 4

5 Do people under stress need advice on which poems to read?
   A No. **B** Yes, they need a doctor's advice.
   C Not if they regularly read poetry.

   | 5

8.7 Talking about pictures   SPEAKING

Unfortunately, in the Speaking paper (Paper 5) you won't be given time to think what to say – and you certainly won't be able to make notes. But the more you practise thinking about what to say and then talking non-stop for a minute, the less difficult this task will seem.

If possible, arrange to do this exercise with another student. If this isn't possible, record your talk using a cassette recorder and a microphone. Then listen to the recording and try to improve your talk.

Imagine that you have been asked this question:

I'd like you to compare and contrast these photographs, saying why you think people enjoy activities like these. Remember, you have only about a minute for this.

Think about what to say (and maybe make some notes).

Working with another student, talk for a minute about the photos.

or **Working alone, record your one-minute talk using a cassette recorder and a microphone. Then listen to the recording and try to improve your talk.**

or **Speaking quietly to yourself, talk for a minute about the photos.**

8.8 Free life membership! WRITING

A

You're keen on joining a health and fitness club, but the annual subscription seems very expensive. You've just seen this advertisement and made the notes on the right. Read the advertisement and your notes on the right carefully.

In Part 1 of the Writing paper (Paper 2) it's important to make sure that you include *all* the relevant points. If you leave any out, you'll lose marks. To make sure you don't forget any points, tick off each point in your notes when you've covered it in the letter.

RENAISSANCE CLUB

Health and fitness for the 21st century

Free membership for life!

It's our tenth birthday this year and to celebrate we're offering free life membership to two lucky people!

If you want to be one of those people, here's what you have to do: Just tell us in about 150 words why you think <u>you</u> should be one of our life members.

Tell us your answers to these questions:
- Why do you value good health?
- Why do you try to keep fit?
- Why do you try to follow a healthy diet?
- How would joining the RENAISSANCE Club change your life?
- Which of these facilities would you use most – and why?

swimming   tennis   basketball   table tennis   weight training

Both winners must agree to feature in our advertising and take part in interviews with the press.

Send your entry and a photo of yourself to Pete Brown, RENAISSANCE Club, PO Box 999.

(Make notes – it may be hard to limit it to 150 words)

(Must answer all the questions – answers needn't be the truth but must sound sincere!)

"give me a new outlook on life" + "chance to make new friends"

(Pick one and explain – it needn't be the truth)

That's fine

Enclosed   (Send a really good photo)

B Write to the Renaissance Club, explaining why you deserve to be chosen (120–180 words).

C Count the number of words you've written. Then compare what you wrote with the Model version on page 103.

LOOKING AFTER YOURSELF

9 Having a great time!

Travel and tourism VOCABULARY

Add the missing words to the puzzle on the right.

1 Fasten your seatbelts and enjoy your … .
2 A travel … sells holidays and makes travel arrangements.
3 It's nice to have a … of things to do on holiday.
4 On an … holiday you don't just lie in the sun, you do things!
5 We drove through the countryside, admiring the … .
6 Taking a … holiday is easier than making all your own travel and accommodation arrangements.
7 At the … you can swim and lie on the beach.
8 It's nice to see the … if you go to a historic city.
9 An … is another word for *outing*.
10 A bed and … is usually cheaper than a hotel.
11 A … flight is cheaper than a scheduled flight.
12 Don't forget your sunscreen if you're going to … .
13 A self-… holiday is cheaper than staying in a hotel.
14 In Paris he bought a little Eiffel Tower as a … .
15 You'll get great views if you go walking in the … .
16 Different holidays are described in a … .
17 (down) You might write this on a postcard! (4 words)

```
                    17
  1 F L I G H T
              2
              3
      4
      5
  6
          7
              8
      9
             10
             11
  12
             13
  14
            15
  16
```

9.2 Adventure holidays READING

Read the brochures on page 47 and find the answers to these questions. Tick the boxes to show the correct answers. (In some cases you should tick two boxes.)

In Part 4 of the Reading paper (Paper 1) you'll have to do an exercise something like this. In this part of the paper you have to look for specific information in the texts. In the exam there will probably be several short texts to read. Base your answers on what the texts say, not what you already know about the subject – they do grow coffee in Costa Rica, but the text doesn't say this.

	Nicaragua	Costa Rica	Neither
1 Which place can you fly directly to from London?	☐	☐	☐
2 In which place can you see dolphins?	☐	☐	☐
3 Which place has volcanoes?	☐	☐	☐
4 Which place is good for bird-watching?	☐	☐	☐
5 Which place has good beaches?	☐	☐	☐
6 Which place has lively nightlife?	☐	☐	☐
7 Which place grows coffee?	☐	☐	☐
8 Which place has historic towns?	☐	☐	☐
9 Which place has few tourists?	☐	☐	☐
10 Which place is popular with painters?	☐	☐	☐
11 Which place is good for looking at fish?	☐	☐	☐
12 Which place is good for buying local arts and crafts?	☐	☐	☐
13 Which place has tropical rain forests?	☐	☐	☐
14 Which holiday includes a trip on a hydrofoil?	☐	☐	☐
15 Which holiday includes travel on a riverboat?	☐	☐	☐

Nicaragua

Beneath the Volcanoes

17 days Hotels/Lodges – Caribbean Escape, Jungles, Colonial Towns

Central America's largest nation is a tropical land of high volcanoes flanked with coffee plantations; exotic flora in dense rainforest; empty, palm-fringed beaches and sleepy old colonial towns – all just waiting to be explored! Peaceful once again, we take the time to uncover some of Nicaragua's special secrets.

Rainforest & Caribbean island

From the ramshackle capital, Managua, we head north to the *Selva Negra* near Matagalpa to walk jungle trails among flowering trees and creeping lianas, looking out for some of Nicaragua's 800 bird species. Then stroll the colonnaded plazas of the old Spanish capital, Leon, before flying to remote Corn Island in the Caribbean sea. Lazy days are spent swimming or snorkelling, offshore a sunken Spanish galleon lies entombed on the reef.

El Castillo – Nelson Retreats

Flying to Bluefields, we make an adventurous journey by boat and road to Juigalpa. Then cruise along the winding San Juan river to El Castillo fortress, where the Spanish forced Lord Nelson to retreat. We'll explore the steam Indo Maiz Rainforest Reserve – our open-sided boat and foot safaris offering us the chance of sighting scarlet macaws, toucans, monkeys and crocodiles. Next we travel to elegant Granada, in the shadow of Mombacho volcano. Horse-drawn carriages clip-clop through the quaint baroque streets, adding to its timeless atmosphere.

Volcanoes & Lake Nicaragua

Two perfect black volcanic cones rise magnificently out of Lake Nicaragua to form Ometepe island – once a burial ground for native indians. There's time to climb Concepcion volcano (1610m), or peer into the lagoon of Maderas crater. Returning to the mainland, we pause at folkloric Masaya, to

browse the native market colourfully stacked with ceramics, naif paintings and basketry.

Itinerary Day 1 Fly London/Managua. **2** Tour of Managua; drive to Matagalpa. **3** In the Selva Negra, birdwatching and trail walks, optional horse riding. **4** Drive to Leon, tour: continue to Managua. **5** Fly to Corn Island; beachcombing, swimming, walks, optional snorkelling. **6** On Corn Island. **7** Fly Bluefields. **8** By boat and bus to Juigalpa, visit museum. **9** Drive to San Carlos; by boat along Rio San Juan to El Castillo; visit fortress. **10** Cruise to Bartola; walks in the Indio Malz Reserve. **11** Birdwatching on foot; boat and hydrofoil to Granada. **12** Sightseeing in Granada; free. **13** Bus then boat to Moyogalpa on Ometepe island. **14** At Moyogalpa; optional ascent of volcano or horseriding. **15** Boat to San Jorge; drive via Masaya market and volcano to Managua. **16** Fly London. **17** Arrive London.

Accommodation & Meals: Hotels RO (11 nts); lodges FB (1 nt) HB (1 nt) RO (2 nts). See p100.

Mode of Travel: Bus/Riverboat/Hydrofoil/On Foot/Flights as itinerary.

Comment: Nicaragua is unused to tourism, so a sense of humour and flexibility are a must. The scenic diversity and friendliness of the people more than compensate.

Group Size: Approx. 12 to 15.

Tour staff and support: Explore Leader plus driver and boatmen.

Ref.CC: Ask for dossier

Costa Rica

Rainforest Adventure

16 days Hotels/Lodges – Rainforest, Wildlife, Volcanoes and Beaches

When Columbus landed at Limon on the Caribbean coast on his fourth and final voyage to the Americas, he could only guess at what beauty the interior possessed. With long sandy beaches, towering volcanoes and unspoilt tropical rainforest, Costa Rica is a naturalist's paradise – the habitat of some 800 species of bird and over 1,200 species of orchid.

Poas Volcano & Guayabo Ruins

Arriving in San Jose, we visit the gigantic Poas volcano (2707 m) – a huge still-smoking crater, where fumeroles are surrounded by tropical forest, and colourful humming birds can be seen hovering among wild orchids. We'll pause at Lankester Gardens near the old colonial capital of Cartago before visiting the ancient Indian ceremonial site at Guayabo, Costa Rica's most important archaeological site.

Tortuguero National Park

After feeling the calypso beat of Caribbean Limon, we make our way into the tangled forests and swamps of Tortuguero National Park. Boarding our riverboat, we'll enter a network of interconnected jungle waterways, where brightly coloured parrots can be seen

among thick creepers and vines. We pause to listen to the cry of howler monkeys or to glimpse the rare manatee.

Monteverde & Pacific Coast

Reaching Puerto Viejo we head for Arenal – a classic volcanic cone that regularly spews out lava and steam. After a boat trip on the Corobici river, we climb into the cloud forest of Monteverde Reserve where some 2,500 species of rare plants are found. Here, we'll enjoy a spot of birdwatching, perhaps catching sight of the unusual bare-necked umbrella bird or even the resplendent quetzal. Finally, we head to Manuel Antonio National Park on the Pacific coast. You can walk among a variety of flora and fauna or just relax on miles of beach, where monkeys and iguanas often come down to the sand.

Itinerary Day 1 Fly London/San Jose. **2** In San Jose, visit Poas volcano, city tour. **3** Drive via Cartago to Turrialba; optional whitewater rafting. **4** Visit Guayabo ruins; drive to Puerto Limon. **5** Drive and boat to Tortuguero National Park. **6** Explorations in Tortuguero N.P. by boat and on foot. **7** Boat to Puerto Viejo. **8** Drive to Arenal area; optional excursion to Tabacon hot springs. **9** Drive to Canas area; lakeside walk. **10** Birdwatching by boat on Corobici river; drive via Arenal to Monteverde Reserve. **11** In Monteverde; walks. **12** Drive via Carara Reserve to Quepos. **13** Visit Manuel Antonio N.P.; walks, relaxing. **14** Drive via Cerro de la Muerta (3490 m) to San Jose. **15** Fly London. **16** Arrive London.

Accommodation & Meals: Hotels RO (5 nts); BB (6 nts); HB (1 nt); lodges FB (2 nts). See p100.

Mode of Travel: Bus/Riverboat/On foot.

Comment: An easy going wildlife exploration with a chance for easy walks in the great outdoors of Costa Rica. Bring lightweight walking boots and a daysac.

Group Size: Approx. 12 to 16.

Tour staff and support: Explore Leader plus driver, boatman and some local guides.

Ref.CC: Ask for dossier

9.3 Spelling and pronunciation – 3: Consonants   WORD STUDY

A

Most of these sentences contain one word which is misspelt. <u>Underline</u> the incorrect word and write it correctly on the right. If there are no mistakes, put a tick (✓) on the right.

Incorrect spelling will lose you marks in the exam, particularly in the Writing paper (Paper 2). 9.3A is similar to Part 4 in the Use of English paper (Paper 3).

1 We had a nasty <u>suprise</u> when the weather changed for the worse.   ...surprise..

2 It's difficult to find cheap accommodation in London.   ....

3 "It's" (with an apostrophe) is short for "It is".   ....

4 I don't know wether you'd like to join me on holiday or not.   ....

5 Please let me know your e-mail adress.   ....

6 APEX is an airline abreviation for an *Advance Passenger Excursion* fare.   ....

7 Please send me a brochure and full infomation about your hotel.   ....

8 They welcomed me cheerfuly and hospitably when I arrived.   ....

9 The doctor gave her patient a thorough examination.   ....

10 My brother has an enormous colection of stamps.   ....

B

All but two of these words are misspelt. Correct the spelling or put a tick.

millionnaire ....   *immensse* ....   *assisstant* ....

exhibition ....   *approximatively* ....   *whisle* ....

knowlege ....   *secondery* ....   *vehicule* ....

height ....   *faught* ....   *dubbled* ....

9.4 *If . . .* sentences – 1   GRAMMAR REVIEW

Make sure that the meaning of your new sentence is as close as possible to the sentence given. Be ready to change the vocabulary as well as the grammar.

Complete the second sentence so that it has a similar meaning to the first sentence, using the word given in bold. You must use between two and five words, including the word given. Don't change the word given.

1 You'll probably enjoy your holiday if it doesn't rain every day.

unless   You're likely to enjoy your holiday ...unless it rains.... every day.

2 I haven't got enough money to travel abroad for my holidays.

afford   If I .... visit other countries on holiday.

3 It's impossible to travel to Russia without a visa.

if   You can't travel to Russia .... a visa.

4 I'm a non-swimmer, so I can't go snorkelling or diving.

swim   If I .... love to go snorkelling or diving.

5 The evenings may be cool, so take a pullover.

in case   I think you should take a sweater .... cool in the evening.

6 My advice is to take traveller's cheques, not cash.

were   If .... take traveller's cheques instead of cash.

7 It may not be necessary for you to help me to pack, I think I can manage by myself.

need   I'll let you know .... help with my packing.

8 It's a good idea to book ahead to be sure of getting a room.

better   You .... you want to get a room.

9 You'll arrive at the airport in the evening, give me a call then.

reach   You don't need to phone me .... the airport.

10 Would Nicaragua or Costa Rica be a better place for a holiday?

prefer   .... Nicaragua or Costa Rica for a holiday?

9.5 Paper 3: Use of English – Parts 1 and 2 Fill the gaps
EXAM TECHNIQUES

A

Read this text and decide which answer A, B, C or D best fits each gap (1–15).

In Part 1 of the Use of English paper (Paper 3), you have to choose one word or phrase from a set of four (A, B, C, D) to fill a gap in a text. The word you choose must have the right meaning and also fit with the grammar in the sentence. Read the text through before you start filling any gaps. In the exam, look at the title of the text and think about what it suggests to you: this will help you to predict what you're going to read, and will help you to understand the text.

Why Explore Worldwide?

For more than 16 years we've pioneered and ¹................... thousands of tours, treks, safaris and expeditions all ²................... the world. Our expertise has ³................... expanded throughout this time, and our continual innovations have kept us at the forefront of adventure ⁴................... . We think of it as a serious and rewarding business, one of life's great ⁵................... . Whichever holiday you choose from our worldwide brochure, we promise you a ⁶................... experience.

Why Small Groups?

We offer a ⁷................... and free-form holiday, loosely-structured for people who reject the horrors of regimentation and mass-produced ⁸................... tours. On most trips our ⁹................... group size is 16 people. That's an ideal number, keeping the experience and enjoyment as personal as ¹⁰................... . Typically, a group consists of about half couples or friends, and about half individuals travelling ¹¹................... . Small groups are environmentally ¹²................... friendly and their effect is less disruptive: they promote a better understanding and awareness among peoples of ¹³................... cultural lifestyles and backgrounds. A small group also means a ¹⁴................... to get away from the crowded tourist haunts to those wild and wonderful ¹⁵................... that excite and capture our imagination.

1 A discovered   B led   C sold   D taken
2 A above   B over   C through   D together
3 A completely   B gradually   C quite   D unexpectedly
4 A excursions   B flights   C journeys   D travel
5 A chances   B experiences   C possibilities   D profits
6 A forgettable   B memorable   C nice   D pleasant
7 A disorganised   B flexible   C long   D short
8 A package   B packaged   C packed   D packet
9 A small   B middle   C probable   D average
10 A ever   B likely   C possible   D usual
11 A alone   B home   C lonely   D together
12 A fairly   B more   C much   D quite
13 A unusual   B similar   C strange   D different
14 A chance   B holiday   C hope   D period
15 A cities   B places   C resorts   D villages

B

Read this text and write down one word which best fits each gap (16–30).

Part 2 of Paper 3 is a 'fill the gaps' text containing fifteen gaps. A single word is needed to fill each gap. In some gaps there may be several possible correct answers – but only write one word. Correct spelling is essential, but using capital letters incorrectly won't lose you marks.

Who Goes with Explore?

Travel is a basic human urge. A chance to discover something new ¹⁶................... ourselves and others. We know that our style of travel appeals to people ¹⁷................... want more out of their holiday ¹⁸................... buckets of cheap wine and a suntan. Typically, the people who go with Explore enjoy ¹⁹................... health, are reasonably active, and want to see the world the way it ²⁰................... be seen. Our brochure includes a ²¹................... range of cultural touring, ethnic encounters, wilderness journeys, seatreks and sailtreks, wildlife safaris, rambles, hikes and treks. So we attract a special ²²................... of person – those prepared to tackle remote or off-beat areas and cope ²³................... the inevitable frustrations. Our trips have no place ²⁴................... rigid attitudes, cultural prejudices or false expectations. Each tour description ²⁵................... you a pretty good idea of ²⁶................... to expect. So choose the trip ²⁷................... works best for you.

Flying Solo?

We're often asked 'Is it okay if I come by myself or will everyone else on the trip ²⁸................... know each other?' It's a fact that our holidays appeal strongly to the single or independent traveller. About half the members of our small groups start out alone. Remember – you're not ²⁹................... a passenger with Explore: everyone joins ³⁰................... . Come alone and you'll soon make friends.

Use the questions on the page to help predict what you'll hear. In the exam you'll get 30 seconds before the recording begins to read the questions through.

9.6 What went wrong?   LISTENING

 Listen to five people talking about their holidays. Choose from the list A–F the experience each speaker describes.

A The airline lost one of the suitcases.

B Someone took the wrong suitcase from the baggage reclaim.

C A suitcase was damaged.

D The hotel was fully booked.

E The room didn't have a sea view.

F The room was very small.

Speaker 1 — 1
Speaker 2 — 2
Speaker 3 — 3
Speaker 4 — 4
Speaker 5 — 5

9.7 A great holiday   SPEAKING AND WRITING

If possible, arrange to do **A** and **B** with another student. If this isn't possible, record your answers to the questions using a cassette recorder and a microphone. Then listen to the recording and try to improve your answers.

A Choose about half a dozen photos from one of your recent holidays – or from a short trip you've taken. If you can't find any photos, then postcards, tickets or even souvenirs will do. Spend a few minutes thinking about how you would answer these questions about them.

Remember that the examiner's aim is to encourage you to talk so that you do provide an adequate sample of your best English for assessment.

Who are the people? What are they doing?
Would you like to be there again now?
What did you not enjoy about that day or place?

What events does this photo remind you of?
What did you enjoy most about that day or that place?
Would you like to go there again? Why / Why not?

B Working with another student, look at each other's photos and ask each other the questions.

or Working alone, record your answers to the questions using a cassette recorder and a microphone. Then listen to the recording and try to improve your answers.

or Speaking quietly to yourself, say what you could say in answer to the questions. Make sure you say more than just a few words in answer to each question.

C Write a letter to a friend about the holiday or trip you talked about in **B** above (120–180 words).

Count the number of words you've written. Then compare your letter with the Model composition on page 103.

In the exam an informal letter is always written for a known reader, such as a pen-friend. In this kind of letter you may have to share an experience or explain your feelings or personal opinions.

Food for thought

10.1 Foods and drinks

VOCABULARY

There are 29 things you can eat or drink hidden in this puzzle. Circle each one you can find. How many drinks are there altogether?

s	a	l	a	d	q	m	p	a	s	t	a	o	j
h	b	t	c	u	c	u	m	b	e	r	o	t	b
r	n	d	t	v	e	g	e	t	a	b	l	e	s
i	b	b	u	t	t	e	r	n	f	r	w	a	x
m	e	a	t	n	c	y	j	h	o	n	e	y	m
p	e	p	p	e	r	t	q	p	o	t	a	t	o
o	r	a	x	s	b	r	e	a	d	u	x	e	k
c	h	e	e	s	e	j	m	p	p	l	e	q	n
w	i	h	g	k	t	u	d	p	b	e	a	n	s
f	f	e	g	m	r	i	d	l	p	i	e	l	a
r	i	c	e	h	v	c	r	e	a	m	f	g	u
u	s	a	l	t	z	e	v	a	c	i	c	b	c
i	h	j	f	h	c	h	o	c	o	l	a	t	e
t	o	m	a	t	o	j	k	b	p	k	u	g	y

10.2 -ing and to . . . – 1

GRAMMAR REVIEW

A Fill each gap with *eating* or *to eat*. (Some of the gaps can take *eating* or *to eat*.)

1 _Eating_ outdoors in summer is pleasant.

2 It's nice .... outdoors in summer.

3 He's very interested in .... exotic foods.

4 I don't feel like .... anything.

5 She doesn't want .... anything.

6 Thanks for inviting me .... with you.

7 I felt sick after .... too much.

8 I dislike .... on my own.

B Complete the second sentence so that it has a similar meaning to the first sentence, using the word in bold. Use between two and five words, including the word given. Don't change the word given.

1 Making breakfast is easier than making dinner.

   difficult It's more _difficult to make dinner than_ it is to make breakfast.

2 I'd prefer a salad to a cooked meal.

   rather I'd .... a cooked meal.

3 A cool, refreshing drink is what I'm hoping to have soon.

   forward I'm .... having a cool, refreshing drink.

4 When I'm on my own I don't bother to cook an elaborate meal.

   worth It's not .... a complicated meal for one.

5 It's not good for your health if you eat too much.

   bad .... for your health.

6 The lights went out and interrupted our meal.

   stopped Everyone .... when the lights went out.

7 Eating out is more expensive than eating at home.

   cheaper It's .... than go to a restaurant.

8 It doesn't take long to squeeze two or three oranges.

   few .... doesn't take long.

10.3 Real cooking   READING

Read this extract from *Real Cooking* by Nigel Slater. For Questions 1–5, choose the answer A, B, C or D which you think fits best according to the text.

In Part 2 of the Reading paper (Paper 1) you have to answer multiple-choice questions on a text. Remember that you have to choose the right answer 'according to the text'. You may have to ignore what you already know about the topic. The writer's opinion may be different from yours.

I passionately believe that anyone can make themselves something good to eat. Cooking is a whole lot easier than many people think. Good cooking – real cooking – is within the grasp of anyone with an appetite and a few pots and pans. There is nothing difficult about it (it is only supper after all), so we can pretty much ignore all that stuff about it being 'an art', 'a science' or 'a gift'.

It takes no expertise to heat some butter and a squashed clove of garlic in a shallow pan till it froths and bubbles, then slide in a piece of chicken. Let it cook till its skin is crisp and golden, then squeeze in half a lemon and serve it with its pan juices and a leafy salad to mop them up. Anyone can slap a lamb chop on a hot grill pan, throw a handful of pasta into bubbling water or put an apple to bake in a hot oven. I work from the not unreasonable assumption that if someone can make a cup of coffee then they can probably roast themselves a chicken.

Real cooking is not about making fancy stocks and sauces, piping purées and perfecting spun-sugar baskets. Real cooking is about making ourselves something to eat that involves a bit of simple roasting, grilling or frying. Nothing complicated. Nothing that is not within the grasp of an inexperienced cook. But it is cooking, rather than opening a packet or a tin. As you will see, real cooking is also about the little things – the small points that turn such straightforward cooking into good cooking. The attention to detail that makes a simple supper into something sublime.

What makes something really good to eat? What is the difference between cooking something that is merely fuel and something that is a joy to eat? It is certainly not the need to make our cooking more complicated, neither is it an art that we must have at our fingertips. It is simply the under-standing of the little things that make something especially good; the golden, savoury, sticky stuff that builds up under a pork chop you have left to cook slowly in its pan; the intense flavour of the bits of lamb that have caught on the bars of the grill; the gravy that you make from the sticky bits left in the pan after you have sautéed some chicken thighs. This is real cooking. The roast potato that sticks to the roasting tin; the crouton from the salad that has soaked up the mustardy dressing; the underneath of the crust of a blackberry and apple pie, rich with purple juice; these are the things that make something worth eating. And worth cooking.

1 The writer believes that …

   A anyone can be a good cook.   **C** cooks need special training.

   B not everyone can be a good cook.   **D** a good cook is an artist.

2 Cooking a chicken requires …

   A more skill than making coffee.   **C** no more skill than making coffee.

   B is easier than making coffee.   **D** is harder than making coffee.

3 The writer prefers …

   A complicated sauces.   **C** simple methods of cooking.

   B food that looks beautiful on the plate.   **D** the food his mother used to make.

4 The difference between simple food and wonderful food is …

   A a great recipe.   **C** taking care what you do.

   B fresh ingredients.   **D** impossible to explain.

5 After you have cooked some meat …

   A wash the pan carefully.   **C** serve it while it's still really hot.

   B taste what's left in the bottom of the pan. **D** let everyone serve themselves from the pan.

10.4 Compound words – 1 WORD STUDY

A

In Part I of the Use of English paper (Paper 3), where you have to fill each gap in a text with one word, there won't be any words with hyphens, but you might have to fill in one word of a two-word compound noun – as in Questions 5–8 of Part A here.

Fill each gap in these sentences with a suitable compound word.

1 I've booked us a table in a ....*first/top*........ -class restaurant.

2 The only way to stay well- .... is to read a newspaper regularly.

3 She gave us each a slice of her delicious old- ....
    home- .... cake.

4 There's nothing more refreshing than .... -squeezed
    orange ....

5 I'd like a glass of .... water, please.

6 We all had food .... from eating undercooked chicken.

7 I need a tin .... if you want me to open this tin.

8 I don't need to see the wine .... I'll just have a bottle
    of the .... wine.

B

In Part 5 of the Use of English paper you'll have to write a single word – not two separate words and not words with hyphens as in B here. Most compound words are not single words, apart from the ones in 11.4 A2 in the Student's Book.

Use the word in bold at the end of each line to form a compound word that fits in the space in the same line.

1 Is someone who is forty .... ? **middle-**

2 If you have .... you don't lose your temper. **self-**

3 I wanted my steak rare not .... **well-**

4 The Eurostar is a .... train. **-speed**

5 A .... flat is less secure than one higher up. **ground-**

6 They aren't rich but they are pretty .... **-off**

7 She's a very .... person. **kind-**

8 He kicks with his left foot because he's .... **left-**

10.5 Five different situations LISTENING

In Part I of the Listening paper (Paper 4) you don't need to understand every word you hear. Just listen carefully for clues to the answers. It's essential to read the questions to find exactly what you have to listen out for.

🔊 Listen to people talking in five different situations. For Questions 1–5, choose the best answer, A, B or C.

1 Two people are in a restaurant. What are they going to drink?
    A wine **B** mineral water **C** tap water
    ☐ **1**

2 Two people are in a restaurant. How much did they pay?
    A £40 **B** £36 **C** £46
    ☐ **2**

3 Two people are preparing a meal. Who is going to make the salad dressing?
    A the man **B** the woman **C** someone else
    ☐ **3**

4 Two people are in a kitchen. What essential ingredient do they *not* have?
    A sugar **B** apples **C** flour
    ☐ **4**

5 Three people are in a restaurant. Which of them is going to pay the bill?
    A the first man (Tim) **B** the second man (Bob) **C** the woman (Ann)
    ☐ **5**

10.6 Prepositions REVISION

Complete the second sentence so that it has a similar meaning to the first sentence, using the word in bold. Use between two and five words, including the word given. Don't change the word given.

1 The stream was very wide and we couldn't get to the other side.

   jump The stream was so wide that we couldn't ..jump across/over........... it.

2 The bus didn't stop at my stop.

   past The bus .... my stop.

3 She approached me with a sarcastic smile on her face.

   came She .... me smiling sarcastically.

4 I can't go to the concert, would you like to have my ticket?

   instead Would you like to go .... me?

5 The dog was barking fiercely as it chased them.

   ran They ...., which was barking fiercely.

6 Bad weather caused the train to be delayed.

   owing The train .... bad weather.

7 I broke the plate by accident, I didn't mean to do it.

   purpose I didn't break .... !

8 When you arrive we'll have finished our meal.

   time .... our meal will be over.

9 Everyone tried to give their orders together.

   time We all tried to order our food ....

10 We didn't expect to meet.

   chance We ....

10.7 Verbs and idioms REVISION

Complete the second sentence so that it has a similar meaning to the first sentence, using the word in bold. Use between two and five words, including the word given. Don't change the word given.

1 Sorry to interrupt you, I'll let you continue working now.

   get Sorry for the interruption, you can .get on with........... your work now.

2 This signature is almost illegible, can you tell whose it is?

   make I can't .... whose signature this is.

3 If you can't think of a true story, use your imagination!

   make If you can't think of a true story, ... !

4 The people in the class treat one another as friends.

   get The members of the class .... each other.

5 I'm not sure what the word means, I'll have to use a dictionary.

   look I'll have to .... before I can tell you its meaning.

6 I wish I had a nice cool drink.

   do I .... a nice cold drink.

7 None of us could understand what he was trying to say.

   getting We couldn't understand what ....

8 I'll come to the station with you and say goodbye.

   see I'll come and .... the station.

9 She didn't want to spend any longer trying to persuade him.

   gave She .... to persuade him.

10 Has he returned the CDs he borrowed from you yet?

   given Has he .... the CDs yet?

10.8 Eating out   SPEAKING

If possible, do these exercises with another student. Alternatively, record your answers to the questions.

 Make notes on what you'd say in response to these questions. Explain your reasons as well as giving your opinions.

1 What is your favourite restaurant or fast food place? What do you like about it?

2 What do you enjoy about eating out? What do you not enjoy? Why?

3 What do you enjoy about cooking? What do you not enjoy? Why?

4 Which of these features are important in choosing a restaurant for a special occasion? Put them in order of importance and explain your reasons:

food   atmosphere   location   friendly staff   price   opening times

 Working with another student, ask each other the questions. Make sure you say more than just a few words in answer to each question.

or Working alone, record your answers to the questions using a cassette recorder and a microphone. Then listen to the recording and try to improve your answers.

or Speaking quietly to yourself, give your answers to each of the questions.

10.9 A birthday celebration   WRITING

 It's your teacher's birthday soon. You and your group want to go out together to his or her favourite restaurant for dinner.

With this kind of task (Part 1 of the Writing paper) (Paper 2) some people think it's a waste of time to make notes. But in the exam it is definitely worth spending just a few minutes making notes. Why is this? Well, making notes helps you to think about what you're going to write and gives you time to think of suitable words and phrases to use in your letter. If you really haven't got time to make notes, at least number the points in the order you're going to make them.

Leo's Restaurant

Today's menu £11.99 for three courses, including VAT and service

STARTERS
- *Avocado with prawns*
- *Home-made pâté*   20 Greek salads instead?
- *Melon and orange salad*

MAIN COURSES
- *Lancashire Hotpot with seasonal vegetables*
- *Steak and kidney pie with new potatoes and vegetables*
- *Cottage pie with seasonal vegetables*
- *Chicken Madras with rice*   for 15
- *Nut and mushroom roast with brown rice*   for 5

DESSERTS
- *Pancakes served with lemon juice and brown sugar*
- *Chocolate mousse*
- *Apple crumble*
- *Blackberry fool*
- *Apple and blackberry pie*   for 20

All our dishes are prepared using the freshest ingredients.

ENJOY YOUR MEAL!

Number in party: 20

Date of party   Friday 12 March

Can't get there before 21.45 — is that OK?
Finish about midnight.

We can only afford £9 per head — If we pre-order our dishes now can we have 3 courses for that? (choices underlined on menu)

Do you have a private room or separate area where we can play music and sing?

One of us in a wheelchair — is access easy?

 Read the menu and your notes below carefully. Write a letter to the restaurant manager (120–180 words), covering all the points in your notes.

C Count the number of words you've written. Then compare your letter with the Model letter on page 103.

11 You never stop learning

11.1 Schools and colleges   VOCABULARY

Add the missing words to the puzzle on the right.

1 Boys and girls attend a … school.

2 Older children attend a … school.

3 Attending school is … up to the age of 16.

4 A young school student.

5 Children start … school at the age of 5.

6 When they're 18, students … school.

7 After school some students go on to … education.

8 Teachers are … of staff.

9 Oxford and Cambridge are famous … .

10 … includes arithmetic, algebra and geometry.

11 Students start in the … at 16 or 17.

12 You have to pay fees at a … school.

13 English and geography are … that all children study.

14 The study of what happened in the past.

15 The person in charge of a school.

16 In the USA older children attend a … … .

17 After school some students go to … to continue studying.

18 Art and music are … in most schools.

19 Schools have to follow the National … .

20 (down) Most children in the UK go to one of these.

11.2 How to do well in exams   READING

In Part 3 of the Reading paper (Paper 3), don't panic if there are words you don't understand. For example, even if you don't understand the words *succinctly* and *stereotypical* in Sentence A, there's enough information in the sentence for you to decide where that sentence fits in the text.

Six sentences have been removed from the article opposite. Choose from the sentences (A–H) the ones which fit in each gap (1–7). There is one extra sentence which you don't need to use.

A Also remember to write legibly and succinctly, and do not be afraid to express the unexpected: after all, examiners can get very bored marking stereotypical answers.

B Close your eyes and take in a few slow, deep breaths to help you relax.

C Do not arrive too early, though, as other people's anxiety can be contagious, and you may suffer from undue panic.

D Go and have a well-earned rest – then prepare for your next exam.

E Map out a quick plan of points you wish to make and how much time you should spend on each question.

F Sleep, exercise and relaxation are all just as important.

G When you get home, read the examination paper through and look up all the words you didn't understand.

H Try not to be tempted to look at those around you, or at the clock.

56

How to ...
... do well in exams

Bet this picture makes you anxious

DO NOT underestimate the power of revision in the days and hours before an examination. The closer you are to the exam, the more chance you have of storing and retaining crucial information. But do not overdo it. **1** F An effective daily routine can help you through an exam period, so in the days leading up to your first exam, get into the habit of being up and ready to work by 9am. It can be a shock to the system after months of working to your own timetable to be mentally alert at that time if you have not prepared for it.

On the day of the exam, have a good breakfast, pack two of everything you need (pens, pencils, erasers, etc.), then make your way to the examination hall in good time. **2**

Once in your seat, simply pause for a few seconds and collect your thoughts. **3** When you turn over the test paper, spend a short period reading through all the instructions and questions, paying particular attention to key verbs such as "discuss", "compare" and "evaluate". **4** It is wise always to allow for 10 minutes at the end of the exam to give yourself time to go back over your answers. Once you have selected the questions you wish to tackle, begin by attempting the one you think is your strongest. It will give you more confidence when you see a well-answered question down on paper. **5**

6 If you do need something else to focus on to help collect your thoughts, choose a fixture in the room, such as the ceiling -- or anything else that will not allow you to be distracted.

Finally, once you have finished, never hang around outside afterwards to attend the inevitable post-mortem by other students. **7**

From the National University of Ireland online examination fact sheet

11.3 *If . . . sentences – 2*   GRAMMAR REVIEW

Complete the second sentence so that it has a similar meaning to the first sentence, using the word in bold. Use between two and five words, including the word given. Don't change the word given.

1 I wasn't able to phone her because I didn't know her phone number.

if I could have phoned her ..*if I had known*.. her phone number.

2 You have to give me the key if you want me to open the door.

unless I can't open the door .... key.

3 We all got wet in the rain.

dry We .... it hadn't rained.

4 It might be colder this evening, so bring a jumper.

case Bring a jumper .... colder this evening.

5 We missed our connection because the train was delayed.

not If the train .... we wouldn't have missed our connection.

6 If he had been nicer to me we might have got on better.

well We didn't .... he was unpleasant to me.

In Part 3 of the Use of English paper (Paper 3) you'll have to fill each gap with 2–5 words – as in 11.3A, but not 11.3B. In the exam *wouldn't* counts as two words (*would not*).

B

Complete the second sentence so that it has a similar meaning to the first sentence. (In this exercise you'll need to use *more* than five words.)

1 I'm not English which is why I have to take this exam.

If I ..*were/was English I wouldn't/would not have to take*.. this exam.

2 My advice to you is this: try to relax before the exam.

If I .... relax before the exam.

3 It was a surprise to meet her there and I was quite embarrassed.

If I .... embarrassed.

4 I may not have time to play basketball tonight, but I hope I will.

If I .... play basketball tonight.

5 I didn't go to the cinema because I didn't finish my supper in time.

If I .... to the cinema.

6 He didn't drive carefully enough, which is why he had an accident.

If he .... an accident.

If you can think of two possible ways of filling a gap, *don't* write them both. You can only get the marks if *both* of them are correct. If one is wrong, you get *no* marks!

11.4 **Compound words – 2**   WORD STUDY

Fill each gap in these sentences with a suitable word.

1 She wears contact lenses because she is short-................................ .

2 I thought they were going to buy a ..*second*..-hand car but they've bought a ..*brand*..-new one.

3 When she won the lottery she put the money into a savings ..*account*.. .

4 Everyone went off to the .... field for a game of football.

5 He's a very good-................................ young man.

6 They decided to save money by booking a last-................................ holiday.

B

In Part 5 of the Use of English paper there will only be one-word compounds like the ones in 11.4B here. Make sure you write the correct singular or plural form if necessary.

Use the word given in capitals at the end of each line to form a word that fits in the space in the same line.

1 The last bus is at midnight according to the .... **TABLE**

2 Go to the dentist if you have .... **TOOTH**

3 Write the vocabulary down in your .... **NOTE**

4 Heathrow, Gatwick and Stansted are London's main .... **AIR**

5 His younger sister is still a .... **SCHOOL**

6 Tom and Bill are both .... **POST**

11.5 **Paper 3: Use of English – Part 4 Correcting errors**
EXAM TECHNIQUES

A

Remember that in this part of the exam, the extra words are most likely to be *grammatical* words:
• articles: *a* or *the*

Follow this procedure.

1 Read the whole text through (including the title) to get the gist before you start writing.

2 Then read the text again, line by line. Put a ring in pencil round the extra words. If you aren't sure, pencil in a question mark and come back to it later.

3 If a line looks OK to you, don't put a tick (✓) immediately. Read it again (or come back to it later) before you commit yourself on the Answer sheet. You can expect about five lines to be correct.

B

• prepositions: *in*, *on*, *with*, etc.
• pronouns: *she*, *it*, etc.
• other grammatical words: *so*, *much*, *some*, *down*, etc.
And not *content* words like *education*, *enjoy*, *continue*, etc.

Read the text below and look carefully at each line. Some of the lines are correct, and some have a word which should not be there. If a line is correct put a tick (✓). If a line has a word which should not be there, write the word in the space. There are two examples (0 and 00).

Lecturer wins $12 million for sex discrimination

0	A former assistant chemistry professor at Trinity College in Hartford, Connecticut has	✓
00	won $12.7 million. Leslie Craine was awarded $671,000 for the lost wages,	the
1	$4 million for emotional distress and $8 million in damages.	
2	"I was astounded at the award," said Ms Craine, aged 55. Jacques Parenteau, her	
3	lawyer, said: "We asked the jury to send out a message that it isn't appropriate to treat	
4	the women differently from men."	
5	She had been in line for a professorship in the organic chemistry at the college when	
6	she was rejected for tenure. A year later she has lost her job.	
7	Ms Craine, who was hired by a department with five male professors, had won	
8	unanimous recommendations in her three evaluations, a teaching award and was	
9	praised for this published work. But the college's tenure review committee rejected	
10	her by 4–1, even although the chemistry department supported her.	
11	Felix Springer, a lawyer was representing Trinity, said that Ms Craine was a fine	
12	teacher but did not produce enough original research. He said that about the	
13	half of the college's teaching staff were women.	
14	He said the college would appeal then. "This was a runaway jury. We don't expect	
15	Trinity will have to pay a dime out."	

11.6 Co-educational or single-sex schools?
SPEAKING AND WRITING

In the Speaking paper (Paper 5), if you can think of any personal experiences to talk about, that's much better than stating general opinions. Describing amusing or memorable events that happened to you are interesting and easier to talk about. In the exam you don't actually have to tell the truth, you can invent imaginary experiences. But don't get carried away – stories about seeing ghosts or solving murders will make you sound strange.

If possible, arrange to do **A** and **B** with another student. If this isn't possible, record your talk using a cassette recorder and a microphone.

A Look at the photos and spend a few moments planning what you can say about them. Don't describe the scenes in detail, just compare and contrast them, using some of the phrases in the speech balloon below.

> One of these pictures makes me think of . . .
> I remember being in a situation just like this once . . .
> This reminds me of the time I . . .
> When I look at the first picture I feel . . . because . . .
> I think the people in the first picture are talking about . . .

B Working with another student, speak for one minute each. Then comment on what your partner said.

or Working alone, speak for about a minute using a cassette recorder and a microphone. Then listen to the recording and try to improve your answers.

or Speaking quietly to yourself, talk about the photos for about a minute.

C Write a composition (120–180 words) giving your opinions on the following statement.

Boys and girls should be educated separately in single-sex schools.

Personal experiences are also interesting in the Writing paper if you have to write an essay or composition giving your opinions.

Make notes before you start writing. Try to support your opinions with some personal examples.

Points for (+ reasons or examples)

Points against (+ reasons or examples)

Conclusion

Count the number of words you've written. Then compare your composition with the Model composition on page 104.

What shall we do this evening?

12.1 Entertainment

There are 25 words connected with the topic of entertainment, television and films hidden in this puzzle. Circle each one you can find.

c	a	g	a	m	e	s	h	o	w	b	d	i
i	h	r	c	u	r	o	c	k	w	p	o	v
n	t	o	h	s	o	c	a	b	l	e	c	a
e	t	v	a	i	m	r	n	e	w	s	u	c
m	h	a	n	c	a	c	r	j	h	e	m	t
a	r	o	n	i	n	a	r	a	o	c	e	o
d	i	r	e	c	t	o	r	z	r	o	n	r
u	l	a	l	e	i	s	w	z	r	m	t	c
b	l	o	a	t	c	c	p	u	o	e	a	r
b	e	f	i	l	m	a	w	a	r	d	r	i
e	r	a	s	t	a	r	b	i	g	y	y	m
d	w	e	s	t	e	r	n	p	a	m	k	e
v	i	d	e	o	b	c	a	r	t	o	o	n

12.2 -ing and to . . . – 2   GRAMMAR REVIEW

Complete the second sentence so that it has a similar meaning to the first sentence, using the word in bold. Use between two and five words, including the word given. **Don't change** the word given.

1 He looked so funny in his new suit that we all had to laugh.

   help   We .... we saw him in his new suit.

2 He said he wouldn't help us.

   refuse   He .... us.

3 She forgot her toothbrush when she was packing.

   remember   She .... pack her toothbrush.

4 I can't concentrate on my work if you talk all the time.

   stop   Please .... I can't concentrate on my work.

5 I agreed to give her a hand with the cooking.

   help   She persuaded .... prepare the meal.

6 They ran and ran until they were worn out.

   went   They .... until they were exhausted.

7 He plays tennis brilliantly.

   good   He .... tennis.

8 I'd like to find out more about the film before I see it.

   interested   I'm .... more about the film before I see it.

12.3 Which film . . . ?   READING

Choose the films (A–F) that match Questions 1–14. For the questions where more than one answer is required, these can be in any order.

Which film . . .

is a love story? **1** ☐ **2** ☐

is a war story? **3** ☐

is about a person who once worked in a school? **4** ☐

is about a woman and a child? **5** ☐

is about a woman who can't do the job she wants to do? **6** ☐ **7** ☐

is about people getting killed? **8** ☐ **9** ☐

is about someone who has run out of ideas? **10** ☐

is about the effects of money? **11** ☐

is funny? **12** ☐ **13** ☐

makes you feel sad? **14** ☐

In Part 4 of the Reading paper (Paper 1) you'll have to read several short texts or a long text divided into several sections. You have to decide which text or section gives you various pieces of information. In the exam there may be as few as four or as many as nine short texts or sections. There are 14 or 15 questions, each worth one mark. (In Parts 1, 2 and 3, where there are fewer questions, each correct answer is worth two marks.)

A Shakespeare in Love
Director: John Madden

Following the award-winning Mrs Brown, John Madden makes Shakespeare accessible with a dream cast and outstanding production design. A romantic comedy set in Elizabethan times, Shakespeare (Joseph Fiennes) is under pressure and has writer's block. Viola (Gwyneth Paltrow) is determined to audition for a role in his new play but is prevented by the law that only men may appear on the stage. In disguise she wins the part of Romeo, but when she meets Shakespeare as herself, they fall in love.

B Notting Hill
Director: Scott Michell

From the screen writer of *Four Weddings and a Funeral, Notting Hill* is a highly entertaining tale of a divorced bookshop owner (Hugh Grant) living in West London. His quiet life is thrown off-track when Anna Scott (Julia Roberts) – the world's most famous film star – walks into his shop. Dealing with the day-to-day details of a love affair, this is a funny and charming romantic comedy.

C Central Station
Director: Walter Salles

A study of the search for family connections, the film follows Dora, an ex-teacher who earns a living at Rio de Janeiro's central station writing letters for the illiterate. When one of her customers is tragically killed moments after dictating a letter, Dora begins a troubled journey taking her and the customer's son into the heart of Brazil. A beautifully crafted, melancholic road movie. (*in Portuguese, with sub-titles*)

D Artemisia
Director: Agnes Merlet

Set in Italy in 1610, Artemisia is the story of a seventeen-year-old girl determined to study art, even though women are not allowed to enter the Academy, let alone study the male form. She persuades her father to let her work on a series of religious frescoes being painted by artist Agostino Tassi. Tassi forces himself on her, and through this violent experience she infuses her work with desire and suffering, going on to achieve greatness. (*in French, with sub-titles*)

E The Thin Red Line
Director: Terrence Malik

Based on the novel by James Jones, the story follows a platoon as they storm the beach of a strategically vital South Pacific island held by the Japanese and then follows their efforts to take the island. A sophisticated and stunningly filmed war epic, placing the audience in the heart of the action, capturing the dread of approach and battle from the soldier's perspective.

F A Simple Plan
Director: Sam Raimi

A Simple Plan is set in the snowy landscape of Minnesota. It is New Year's Eve when two brothers and their friend stumble across the wreckage of a small plane with a dead pilot and $4 million in used notes aboard. They plan to keep the money until it is safe to spend it but the plan goes wrong in a sea of greed, paranoia, distrust and bloodshed.

12.4 Using suffixes – 1: Adjectives   WORD STUDY

A Form adjectives from these words, using the suffixes below.

-able   -al   -ical   -ish   -y   -less   -ful

nation ....*national*.........   child ....   fog ....

accident ....   history ....   delight ....

success ....   region ....   forget ....

education ....   pain ....   hope ....

B Form adjectives from these words to complete the sentences below.

admire   comfort   draught   fashion   job   rely   speech   tact

1 I don't like this chair, it's very ....

2 Another word for *unemployed* is ....

3 I like your new shoes! They're very ....

4 I didn't know what to say, I was completely ....

5 Please shut the window, it's very .... in here.

6 You can never trust him, he's completely ....

7 I think it's .... that he's always ready to help others.

8 She upsets people rather a lot because she's rather ....

12.5 What did you think of it?   LISTENING

In this kind of listening exercise it's sometimes easy to jump to the wrong conclusions. Look carefully at the alternatives and listen to the whole of each conversation. Don't assume your first impression is correct – there may be more important information at the end of the conversation.

🔊 **Listen to people talking in five different situations. Choose the best answer A, B or C for each question.**

1 Two people are talking. What are they talking about?
   A a film   **B** a TV programme   **C** a concert   **1** ☐

2 Two people are talking. What do they decide to do this evening?
   A go to the cinema   **B** go to a friend's house   **C** rent a video at home   **2** ☐

3 Two people are at a concert. What was annoying them?
   A watches beeping   **B** people coughing   **C** mobile phones   **3** ☐

4 Two people are at a cinema. Why can't they see the film?
   A They're too late.   **B** It's not on this week.   **C** There are no seats.   **4** ☐

5 Three people are talking. Who enjoyed the evening least?
   A the first man (Frank)   **B** the woman (Liz)   **C** the second man (Tony)   **5** ☐

12.6 Paper 3: Use of English – Part 3 Rewriting sentences
EXAM TECHNIQUES

Part 3 of the Use of English paper tests grammar and vocabulary. A wide range of structures such as reported speech, passive voice, conditionals, verb tenses as well as modal verbs are tested. In addition, phrasal verbs and lexical phrases such as *to have difficulty in -ing*, *to take notice of*, *to look forward to -ing*, etc., can be tested in this format.

Each answer in Part 3 is worth 2 marks. If you get half of the answer right you get 1 mark.

Before you do the test below, look at these *Dos* and *Don'ts* for Part 3 of Paper 3:

- Don't change the word given. It must stay **exactly** the same.
- Don't change the meaning of the sentence (but you may have to change the style or emphasis slightly).
- Don't write more than five words. Or fewer than two.
- Remember that *don't* and *isn't* count as two words.
- Write legibly. If the examiner can't read every word, you'll lose marks.
- Make sure your spelling is correct. Incorrect spelling loses marks.
- Check that you've written only the missing words on the Answer sheet.

Part 3

For Questions **31–40**, complete the second sentence so that it has a similar meaning to the first sentence, using the word given. **Do not change the word given.** Use between two and five words, including the word given. Write only the missing words **on the separate answer sheet**.

31 I'm sorry that I stayed up so late last night.
    wish
    I .... to bed earlier last night.

32 I wonder what her name is.
    like
    I .... her name.

33 Gloria didn't try to phone Bill again.
    gave
    Gloria .... Bill.

34 Bob said to us, "Don't make so much noise."
    not
    Bob .... so much noise.

35 I think you should send them a Thank You letter.
    better
    You .... a letter to thank them.

36 We were friends when we were at school and we are still friends.
    since
    We .... were at school together.

37 It's unusual for Tim to be late.
    hardly
    Tim .... late.

38 I can't afford such expensive tickets.
    too
    Those tickets are .... buy.

39 I knew what to do because, luckily, I'd read the instructions.
    not
    I wouldn't have known what to do .... the instructions.

40 These days fewer vegetables are eaten than in the past.
    many
    People these days don't .... they used to.

Part 3	
31	
32	
33	
34	
35	
36	
37	
38	
39	
40	

12.7 Which prize would you choose? SPEAKING

If possible, arrange to do this exercise with another student. If this isn't possible, record your answers to the questions using a cassette recorder and a microphone.

A Imagine that you have entered a competition and the first prize is one of the things described and illustrated here. Decide which prize you would choose and explain why. Think about what you might say before you move on to **B**.

In Part 3 of the Speaking paper (Paper 5) you'll take part in a three-minute *Collaborative task* with the other candidate. This discussion is based on photos or illustrations. There is no need to complete the task and actually make a decision. Marks are awarded for the way you speak to each other and involve each other in the discussion. Encourage the other candidate to say what he or she thinks. It's OK to interrupt politely if you want to say something.

FIRST PRIZE: *Your choice ...*

✳ a personal MiniDisc player

✳ a personal CD player

✳ a pair of tickets for the opera

✳ a one-month pass for the cinema

✳ a personal DVD player

✳ a laptop computer

✳ a meal for eight at the best restaurant in town

✳ a weekend for two at a five-star hotel by the sea

B Working with another student, talk about the options together. Make sure you give each other a chance to speak, using some of the phrases below.

or Working alone, record your views using a cassette recorder and a microphone. Then listen to the recording and try to improve your answers.

or Speaking quietly to yourself, give your views.

> What do you think?
> Sorry, can I just interrupt?
> I don't really agree with you about that.
>
> Do you agree?
> Just a moment, I'd like to say that ...
> I'm not sure that I agree with you.

12.8 I'm sorry you missed the end ... WRITING

You went to the cinema with a friend. Your friend had to leave half-way through and missed the second half of the film. Write your friend a letter (120–180 words) reminding him or her what happened in the first half and then telling him or her what happened in the end. (Write about a film you remember well and which you enjoyed.) Count the number of words you've written. Then compare your composition with the Model letter on page 104.

13 Read any good books?

Books and magazines   VOCABULARY

Add the missing words to the puzzle on the right.

1 I like a book which has a good … .
2 A list of the chapters and what they contain.
3 What's written on the back of a book.
4 A book with an exciting story.
5 Novels and stories are works of … .
6 Shakespeare's plays are … .
7 This new book got a good … in the paper.
8 The story of a book or film.
9 A person who writes books.
10 The people in a story.
11 A place you can borrow books from.
12 The name of a book.
13 Can you … me that book when you've finished it?
14 A book telling the story of someone's life.
15 A list of difficult words with explanations.
16 The front of a book.
17 A place where you can buy books.
18 (down) Of all the books you've read, which is … … … ? (3 words)

Crossword puzzle. 1 across answer shown: STORY

13.2   **When do you read?**   LISTENING

Listen to five people talking about their reading habits. Choose from the list A–F what each speaker says. There is one extra letter you don't need to use.

A Reading in bed sends me to sleep.

B I used to read a lot, but not any more.

C I haven't read a book since I was at school.

D I read when I'm on the train to work.

E I only read when I'm on holiday.

F I always read in bed.

Speaker 1		1
Speaker 2		2
Speaker 3		3
Speaker 4		4
Speaker 5		5

13.3 Joining sentences – 1: Relative clauses   GRAMMAR REVIEW

Join these pairs of sentences beginning with the words given. Make sure you put the commas in the right places. (You'll need to write *more* than five words in these sentences.)

1 A man phoned and asked for you. He spoke with a foreign accent.

   The man .... foreign accent.

2 Ruth Rendell writes crime stories. She also writes under the name Barbara Vine.

   Ruth Rendell .... crime stories.

3 Jay Gatsby is the main character in the book. He is a millionaire.

   Jay Gatsby .... in the book.

4 John le Carré writes spy stories. His real name is David Cornwell.

   John le Carré .... spy stories.

5 Michael Crichton wrote *Jurassic Park*. He used to be a hospital doctor.

   Michael Crichton .... *Jurassic Park*.

6 John Grisham is one of the world's best-selling authors. He was a lawyer before he became a writer.

   John Grisham .... best-selling authors.

7 *The Night Manager* was written by John le Carré. It's about a man who works in a hotel.

   John le Carré .... in a hotel.

8 I enjoy reading books. I particularly enjoy reading thrillers.

   The kind of .... thrillers.

13.4 Using suffixes – 2: Actions and people   WORD STUDY

What do you call someone who ... ?

performs	a *performer*	plays a piano	a ....
participates	a	supervises	a ....
plays a guitar	a	invents things	an ....
narrates a story	a		
employs people	an		
observes	an		
takes photographs	a		
writes novels	a		
assists people	an		

B

Use the word in bold at the end of each line to form a word that fits in the space.

1 I was surprised when she .... her tea with honey instead of sugar.   **sweet**

2 We were .... when the lightning struck the house next door.   **terror**

3 She is sensitive about her work and hates being ....   **critic**

4 After a dull morning, the weather .... in the afternoon.   **bright**

5 I know I'm .... but I think Americans are very friendly people.   **general**

6 The road was .... to take an extra lane of traffic.   **wide**

7 The UK has over 25 million foreign .... a year.   **visit**

8 A .... is someone who studies plants and animals.   **biology**

Cambridge English Readers

READ ANY GOOD BOOKS?

Five clauses have been removed from the blurbs below. Choose from the clauses (A–F) the ones which fit in each gap (1–6). There is one extra clause which you don't need to use.

These extracts are from Cambridge English Readers, a new series of original fiction, specially written for learners of English.

A does not know what to do

B finds herself drawn into a mystery

C is suddenly called back to London on business

D it is too hot to go out

E sets out to free them

F takes up golf

Dolphin Music
Antoinette Moses

The year is 2051. CONTROL, the government of Europe, keeps everyone happy in a virtual reality. This is a world where **1** and where wonderful music made by dolphins gives everyone pleasure. It's a world which is changed forever when music critic Saul Grant discovers what makes dolphins sing and **2** .

Nothing but the Truth
George Kershaw

Hu is a teenage student at an international school in the exciting city of Bangkok. She has a problem with one of the teachers and **4** . An adventure in a national park, acting in a musical, and the help of friends make Hu realise that she must tell nothing but the truth.

When Summer Comes
Helen Naylor

Stephen and Anna Marins take a holiday break in a seaside village to escape the stress of London. They love it there and make a new friend, a local fisherman. But when Stephen **3** , their lives start to change.

Death in the Dojo
Sue Leather

Reporter Kate Jensen is investigating the death of a karate master in a 'dojo', a karate training room, in London. Another death quickly follows and Jensen **5** that leads her to Japan, and to a crime committed thirty years earlier.

Three sentences have been removed from each extract opposite. Choose from the sentences (A–P) the ones which fit in each gap (1–12). There is one extra sentence for each extract which you don't need to use.

Even if you aren't studying a background reading text, reading a story in English is an enjoyable way of revising English, reminding you of vocabulary and exposing you to some new vocabulary. Try a reader at level 4 or 5 in the Cambridge English Readers series!

A Saul Grant's computer spoke with a Scottish accent.

B He found writing difficult and hated to be interrupted.

C He had been working for too long today.

D He liked writing and found it difficult to think and talk at the same time.

E Everyone thought the heat would only last for a few days and then the rain would return, but this summer was different.

F Anna and Stephen loved hot weather.

G People were not used to high temperatures day after day.

H It was the hottest summer for twenty years.

I It was a cool January morning, the first day of the spring term.

J There was light in the sky now, a soft orange light in the grey dawn.

K It was time for Hu to get up.

L It was not yet six o'clock.

M This is a newspaper for the Twenty-first century – we want facts, not fantasy.

N Then you get a train to safety.

O Then down and into the cold night air.

P You're wasting your time.

Chapter 1 *Life was good*

Tuesday 27 May, 2051. 2 p.m. Richmond, England.

'We have been working on blue with black letters for three hours, five minutes and twenty five seconds.' **1** 'We will now change to black and white for one hour.' 'OK,' Saul told the machine. He yawned and rubbed his red eyes. **2** His computer knew that. His computer knew everything. It knew Saul's voice and Saul could talk to it if he wanted to. But he did not like talking to his computer. **3** He did not know why, but he did know that many of the Web writers had the same problem.

Saul Grant was a writer. He was a music critic for the Central England Web Guide. He loved music and he loved writing about music. Many people wanted his job, but he was good at it and his bosses were pleased with him.

But next week he had to stop writing and do six months of community work. Saul hated community work. Everyone had to do it. Saul knew that. There were too many people and too few jobs

Chapter 1 *The city heat*

'When we get to Polreath on Saturday, I'm going to do nothing,' said Anna. 'I just want to sit and have cool drinks and read and watch the world go by.'

'Me too,' replied Stephen.

4 It had started at the end of May. **5**

'And don't expect any intelligent conversation from me,' Anna continued. 'It'll take a day or two for me to become a member of the human race again!'

'Mm,' said Stephen, not really listening. 'What about this cottage we've booked, do you think it's going to be all right? To be honest, I'm a bit worried about it – we were so late making our decision and it was still available. Why didn't anyone else want it! It makes me think there must be something wrong with it.'

'Don't worry. I'm sure it'll be fine. And even if it's not, we'll still be away from here. Just think – three weeks by the sea, without any work. It sounds wonderful.'

In the city the heat was uncomfortable. **6** Journeys to work became hot and sweaty, and increasingly bad-tempered in the crowded trains and buses. By the beginning of July, nobody could remember when it had last rained

Chapter 1 *Dawn in Bangkok*

Hu decided to get up. She couldn't sleep. The first bird of the Bangkok dawn, the cuckoo, started its noisy, morning cry, '*Gow-wow! Gow-wow!* Get up! Get up!' Hu could hear the growing noise of the early morning traffic. **7**

It was impossible to sleep. She walked over to her window and opened it. The noise and the smell of the big city washed over her. It was still dark. **8**

Hu looked out of the window. The newspaper man arrived on his motorbike and gave his parcel of newspapers to the man at the entrance of the apartment block. The two men laughed, and then the newspaper man waved and drove noisily away to the next apartment block in the Soi, the next street. **9**

It was always difficult to sleep the night before the new term, but this time it was even harder. Hu was excited. She would see Marwa and Thomas and Yoshiko again, and that was exciting. She would do less housework and more school work, and that was exciting too

Chapter 1 *Death of a fighter*

'You kill the guy with a karate punch to the left kidney. Yaku zuki – reverse punch. You step over the body lying on the wooden floor, take one last look at the face, eyes still open in an expression of surprise, and move quickly through the door of the dojo to the lift.

10 You almost allow yourself to smile as you walk towards the Underground station, your right hand still aware of the contact with Kawaguchi-sensei's body. **11** '

'Cut the poetry, Jensen. **12** ' This was the sweet voice of my boss, Dave Balzano, editor of The Daily Echo, as he looked over my shoulder at my computer screen.

'Yes, sir,' I said under my breath as he moved on towards his office. Balzano was a fat, sweaty man with a bad temper. I had learnt from bitter experience that there was no point in arguing with him. I looked again at what I had written.

'Pity,' I whispered to my colleague, Rick. 'I quite like it.' Rick smiled but carried on looking at his screen.

Rick and I were both news reporters on The Daily Echo. I had been working there for about three years and Rick joined about a year after me. Like me, he had started off on a less well-known newspaper outside London

13.6 **Paper 2: Writing – Part 2** EXAM TECHNIQUES

First read this advice.

Whenever you write a composition, try to do it in 40 minutes.

Before you start writing, you should …
- Read all the questions and decide which one to answer (2–3 minutes).
- Make notes (3–5 minutes).

Then …
- Write your composition. Leave a wide margin and a couple of lines between each paragraph. Write neatly in the exam. Difficult-to-read handwriting may put the examiner in a bad mood.

Then allow an extra 5 minutes to …
- Count the approximate number of words (1 minute). Count the number of words in an average line and multiply this by the number of lines you've written. Aim to write about 150 words every time.
- Check your work for mistakes in spelling and grammar.
- Make any corrections necessary.
- If you've written more than 180 words, find a sentence to delete.

> Even if you have read a set text, you don't have to answer a question in the Writing paper unless you want to. Read all the questions in Part 2 carefully – you may find that one of Questions 2–4 suits you better than Question 5.

Note down the time on your watch. Now choose *one* of these compositions. Make notes first and then write your answer in 120–180 words in an appropriate style.

> Don't get too worried about writing in an appropriate style. As long as you're aware of the difference between a friendly style and a more formal style that's fine. In these compositions, 2 and 3 are friendly and 4 is more formal.

2 Your rich uncle and aunt paid for you to go on holiday. Write them a letter telling them about the holiday and thanking them for their generosity.

Write your **letter**.

3 You have decided to enter a short story competition. The rules say that the story must begin with these words:

I know it's hard to believe but …

Write your **story**.

4 You have a Saturday job in a shop that sells books and magazines. Not many young people come into the shop. The owner has asked you to suggest some ways of attracting more young people.

Write a **report** for the owner.

5 Answer **one** of the following questions based on your reading of one of the set books. Your answer should contain enough detail to make it clear to someone who may not have read the book. Write (**a**) or (**b**) as well as the number **5** in the question box, and the **title** of the book next to the box.

Either (a) Do you think that reading a simplified edition of a book in English is a good experience? Or do you get a better experience by reading a translation of a book in your own language?

Write a **composition** giving your views with reference to the book which you have read.

Or (b) Write a letter to a friend encouraging him or her to read the book you have read, explaining what you enjoyed most about the book.

Write your **letter**.

Before you compare your answer with the Model answer on page 104, follow the last four tips in Ⓐ.

All in a day's work

14.1 Jobs and employment   VOCABULARY

There are 25 words connected
with work hidden in this puzzle.
Circle each one you can find.
(Ignore any words that are not
connected with the topic of work.)

s	t	a	f	f	p	r	o	f	i	t	p	e
a	t	r	a	i	n	i	n	g	w	p	r	m
l	e	m	a	i	l	a	p	p	l	y	o	p
a	p	r	o	f	e	s	s	i	o	n	m	l
r	c	k	f	a	c	t	o	r	y	q	o	o
y	a	d	e	p	a	r	t	m	e	n	t	y
a	f	i	n	t	e	r	v	i	e	w	i	e
s	i	t	o	f	f	i	c	e	p	o	o	r
w	r	f	i	r	e	s	a	c	k	o	n	e
a	m	a	n	a	g	e	r	e	t	i	r	r
g	a	s	p	j	o	p	e	n	s	i	o	n
e	m	p	l	o	y	e	e	a	b	o	s	s
s	i	c	k	b	i	g	r	e	t	i	r	e

14.2 Joining sentences – 2: Conjunctions   GRAMMAR REVIEW

Complete the second sentence so that it has a similar meaning to the first sentence, using the
word in bold. Use between two and five words, including the word given. Don't change the
word given.

1 We had a very bad trip and we spent the next day recovering.

   such We had .... it took us a day to recover.

2 In spite of having a terrible headache she went to work all the same.

   although She went to work .... headache.

3 The last time I played cards was during my last holiday.

   since I .... my last holiday.

4 I made notes because I wanted to remember everything.

   so I made notes .... remember everything.

5 He felt very nervous at the interview but he got the job.

   despite He got the job .... at the interview.

6 He lost his job and then he had more time for his hobbies.

   after He had more time for his hobbies .... job.

7 She had good qualifications but she didn't even get an interview.

   even She wasn't called for an interview .... well-qualified.

8 She was very happy when she got the job and spent the night celebrating.

   so She was .... getting the job that she celebrated all night.

At Last I Have Time!   R E A D I N G

Read the article and choose from the alternatives A–E to answer questions 1–10. The alternatives may be chosen more than once.

A The Happy Unemployed	**D Guillaume Paoli**
B Politicians	**E A woman from Koblenz**
C A man from Aachen	

Match the person or group (A–E) to these statements.

1 A company with fewer workers is more profitable.

2 Being offered work is annoying.

3 Having no job gives more time for leisure and artistic activities.

4 I haven't worked for four years.

5 It would be good if more people had jobs.

6 People have to make others believe that they to want to find work.

7 The government is putting too much pressure on the unemployed.

8 Unemployed people should get money for letting work-lovers work.

9 Unemployed people shouldn't be ashamed of not having work.

10 Unemployment is good for the economy.

Happy jobless laugh off the German work ethic

Denis Staunton in Berlin

WORKSHY* of the world unite: you have nothing to lose but your shame. That's the message from a German pressure group, the Happy Unemployed.

While politicians argue about how to get 4 million jobless Germans back to work, these unemployed Berliners are claiming that they are doing the state a favour by doing nothing.

Since publishing its manifesto a few weeks ago, the group has received hundreds of letters from unemployed people who fear that an improvement in the country's economy could force them back into work. For many, life began the moment they lost their job.

"I've learnt to paint and compose music on my computer. I've become creative and go to parties. I need time because I have one girlfriend in Cologne and another in Düsseldorf," a man from Aachen wrote.

The manifesto, At Last I Have Time, argues that the unemployed are forced to pretend that they want to work because of pressure from their friends.

According to founder Guillaume Paoli, aged 39, the real difficulty unemployed people face is pressure from the authorities to look for work. "The obligation to work is a big problem." He believes the happily unemployed should be rewarded for leaving jobs free for those who enjoy work. He claims that the economy requires a certain level of unemployment to keep inflation low and argues that, since the stock market rewards companies that lay off staff, sacked workers often generate more profit than those who remain employed.

But the authorities show no sign of leaving the workshy in peace, as an unemployed woman from Koblenz wrote in the group's magazine. "For the past four years I have been happily out of work, or 'free of work' as I call it," she wrote. "Unfortunately, my happiness is disturbed time and again by the employment office."

* Workshy = people who dislike work and try to avoid it

14.4 Using suffixes – 3: Abstract nouns   WORD STUDY

A Write down the noun from these adjectives.

accurate	_accuracy_	simple	
efficient		shy	
able		generous	
patient		bored	
proud		anxious	
frequent		hungry	
arrogant		thirsty	
brilliant			

B Use the word in bold at the end of each line to form a word that fits in the space.

1 His .... is not very good. **pronounce**

2 I don't know why they did it, their .... were incredible. **explain**

3 Is the age of .... 60 or 65? **retire**

4 The audience expressed their .... by booing and whistling. **approve**

5 Pollution threatens the .... of endangered species. **survive**

6 You can't write a story without using your .... **imagine**

7 Films, TV, music are different kinds of .... **entertain**

8 At an airport there are separate screens for .... **arrive**

and .... **depart**

14.5 Having fun at work   LISTENING

In the exam, you hear each recording twice. If you aren't sure of an answer the first time, write a guess in pencil or leave a blank. Then listen carefully for the information the next time. The questions are in the same sequence as the information given in the recording.

Listen to the radio programme and fill in the missing information in the spaces.

Having fun at work leads to: [   ] **1**

When did Virgin start its financial services group? [   ] **2**

Richard Branson likes a joke and doesn't take himself too [   ] **3**

Creativity doesn't flourish in companies where people [   ] **4**

Encouraging creativity in a company means involving [   ] **5**

It's easier to be creative in a small, new company than a [   ] **6**

For creativity to flourish there has to be an atmosphere of [   ] **7**

And people must have time to [   ] **8**

It's not easy to be creative if you're under [   ] **9**

Today's successful companies depend on [   ] **10**

and [   ] **11**

Creativity will separate the winning companies from [   ] **12**

14.6 **Paper 5: Speaking** EXAM TECHNIQUES

If possible, arrange to do **B** and **C** with another student. If this isn't possible, record your answers to the questions using a cassette recorder and a microphone.

Look at page 113 in the Student's Book and read the description of the Speaking paper.

PART 1 (3 minutes)	The examiner asks you and the other candidate about yourselves. (you're going to practise this in 14.6B)
PART 2 (4 minutes)	One-minute uninterrupted talks about two photos, followed by a short discussion. (you practised this in 5.7, 8.7 and 11.7)
PART 3 (3 minutes)	Look at the pictures and discuss a problem-solving task with the other candidate. Then you …
PART 4 (4 minutes)	… discuss the topic of the pictures with the other candidate. The examiner asks you questions to encourage you both to give your opinions. (you practised this in 12.7)

What if you're paired with another candidate who tries to dominate the conversation and won't give you a chance to speak?

The examiners are trained to make sure that you get a chance to speak too. But don't rely on this: interrupt the other candidate (politely) if you want to say something.

B

In Part 1 (3 minutes) the examiner asks you and your partner about yourselves. You may be asked *some* questions like these. Decide what you can say in answer to each one. Try to say more than just *Yes* or *No*.

Let's begin with your home town (or village).

- Where are you from?
- Can you tell me about your home town?
- What is there to do in the evenings?
- What part of the town do you like most and why?

And what about your family?

- Do you have a large or small family?
- Can you tell me something about them?

And what about you?

- Can you tell me something about yourself?
- Do you work or are you a student?
- What do you enjoy most about your work/studies?
- What qualifications did/will you need for your job/the job you hope to do?

What do you do in your spare time?

- Do you have any hobbies?
- How did you become interested in that?
- Which do you prefer more: watching TV or going to the cinema?
- What sort of programmes/films do you like to watch?
- What kind of music do you enjoy most? How do you usually spend your holidays?
- Is there anywhere you'd like to visit? Why?

What are your future plans?

- What do you hope to do in the next few years?
- How important is English for your future plans?
- What do you hope to be doing in five years' time?

What if you're paired with another candidate who doesn't reply when you ask his or her opinion?

The examiners are trained to intervene to make the exam fair for both of you. But don't rely on this. If you are kind and polite to the other candidate and encourage him or her to speak you will get extra marks.

What if you're paired with someone you don't get on with or dislike?

Don't let this influence you during the exam. Try to behave as if you like each other!

C

Working with another student, ask each other the questions. Make sure you say more than just a few words in answer to each question.

or **Working alone, record your answers to the questions using a cassette recorder and a microphone. Then listen to the recording and try to improve your answers.**

or **Speaking quietly to yourself, give your answers to each of the questions.**

If you don't understand the examiner – or the other candidate – don't hesitate to ask for clarification. Be natural!

14.7 A summer job　　WRITING

A

You're keen on getting a part-time job during the summer.
You've just seen this advertisement and made the notes on the right.

> Remember that it's important to include all the relevant information and not to put in any irrelevant information in this sort of letter. Check your work through to make sure you haven't missed anything out.

SUMMER BEACH ASSISTANTS

We are looking for beach assistants for the summer season. Successful applicants will be friendly, reliable and fit people who will spend most of their time dealing with members of the public.

Duties include:

- Moving sunbeds, beach umbrellas and pedalos.
- Taking money for sunbeds, beach umbrellas and pedalos.
- Giving information to beach users from different countries. (Knowledge of English essential. Other languages also an asset.)
- Cleaning the beach morning and evening.

Please apply in writing to:

Beach Superintendent, Beach Office, Seatown, ST8 9DN

I enjoy talking to people.

Say which languages I can speak.

I don't mind physical work.

Describe myself (age, education, etc.).
Ask about pay + dates.

B Read the advertisement and your notes on the right carefully. Then write a letter to the Beach Superintendent, applying for the job (120–180 words).

C Count the number of words you've written. Then compare your letter with the Model letter on page 105.

"Actually, I'm just down here on business."

15 Can you explain?

Technology and science   VOCABULARY

Add the missing words to the puzzle on the right.

1 The study of matter and natural forces.
2 The study of the elements.
3 The study of living things.
4 CO_2 is a ... consisting of one atom of carbon and two of oxygen.
5 Scientists carry these out to test their theories.
6 Use these for cutting.
7 Use this to tighten a screw.
8 Scientists work here.
9 Read the ... book before you operate the machine.
10 A can opener is a useful ... .
11 Press this ... to turn the TV on.
12 All machines ... ... eventually –
13 – but not so often if they are ... regularly –
14 – at least that's probably true in ... .
15 He or she makes things from wood.
16 I can't find the TV ... control.
17 The TV's on very loud. How do you adjust the ... ?
18 A desktop computer has one, but a laptop doesn't.
19 Use this to stick things together.
20 Every computer has one of these.
21 (down) What this unit is about. (3 words)

```
                        21
              1  P H Y S I C S
                  2
                  3
              4
         5
                  6
                  7
                  8
                  9
              10
              11
              12
         13
                 14
         15
              16
              17
              18
                 19
              20
```

15.2 **The Swiss Army Knife**   READING

Six sentences have been removed from the article opposite. Choose from the sentences (A–H) the ones which fit in each gap (1–7). There is one extra sentence which you don't need to use.

A Wenger, for example, offers Swiss Army watches.

B Victorinox says it makes 'the original Swiss Army Knife'.

C He won the contract to supply the standard knife for the army but had to share it with another Swiss company.

D Then Karl Elsener, the fourth son of a Swiss hat-maker, decided to become a knife-maker.

E It included a Swiss Army Knife.

F 12 million Swiss Army Knives are sold every year.

G Officers preferred – and were prepared to pay for – a lighter version with six functions.

H They have been used during Arctic expeditions, on Everest climbs and in the White House.

Brand values: Swiss Army Knife

By Nicholas Bannister

When billions of pounds are thrown at a project, it is often the little things that get overlooked.

In the early 1990s, when the US space shuttle Columbia was launched at huge cost, an important piece of equipment needed to be fixed, but none of the tools provided fitted. A crew member had his trusty Swiss Army Knife and one of its many screwdrivers did the job.

The Swiss Army Knife, for all its military connections, is not an offensive weapon but a pocket toolkit.

The Swiss decided in 1886 to issue all their army recruits with a knife but had to import them from Solingen in Germany because there was no local manufacturer. **1**

After learning the trade in Germany, he returned to Switzerland and set up a factory in Ibach, bringing much-needed industrial work to a rural part of his homeland. **2**

To this day, Victorinox, Elsener's company based in German-speaking Switzerland, and Wenger, in the French-speaking part of the country, share the right to make the Swiss Army Knife.

The companies distinguish their products with slight differences in wording which acknowledge Elsener's initiative. **3** Wenger says it makes 'the genuine Swiss Army Knife'.

While young soldiers in Switzerland's army get a standard knife free, officers have to buy their own – a situation that is responsible for the multi-tooled knife so widely known today.

4 Today it is the officers' knife, with up to 33 tools, which is best known.

The officer knife was patented on June 12, 1897. Years later, the New York Museum of Modern Art included its successor, the SwissChamp Knife, in its collection.

Demand for the knife has long outstripped Swiss army requirements. More than 90% of the knives are exported and are popular gifts throughout the world. **5** US President Lyndon Johnson used to present Swiss Army Knives engraved with his initials to official guests, a tradition continued by Ronald Reagan and George Bush.

It was American servicemen who were largely responsible for making the Swiss Army Knife an international icon when they bought them from US forces' stores around the world between 1945 and 1949. When the Russians shot down the U2 spy plane piloted by Gary Powers in the 1960s, sparking an international crisis, they published a list of all the pilot's equipment. **6**

Today Victorinox alone makes about 34,000 Swiss Army Knives a day and offers about 100 different tool combinations.

But the popularity of the Swiss Army Knife has created a brand-name which the manufacturers use for other products. **7**

Removing stones from horses' hooves is no longer a high priority for Swiss Army Knife owners. But bottle and can openers, wire strippers, screwdrivers, tweezers, nail files, corkscrews, scissors, wire cutters, magnifying glass, chisels and even watches are among the many options for the modern user.

15.3 Using the passive GRAMMAR REVIEW

Fill each gap in this text with the correct form of the verbs on the right. Use one or two words in each gap. Although some of the gaps need a passive form, some don't! (In the exam you only have to write one word.)

The story of Velcro

Velcro [1]................. in 1948 when a Swiss engineer, Georges de Mestral, [2].................   invent take
his dog for a walk in the country. After the walk de Mestral [3]................. that his dog   find
and his own trousers [4]................. with sticky burrs. This [5]................. him wonder   cover make
why they [6]................. themselves to his clothes.   attach

When the burrs [7]................. under a microscope de Mestral [8]................. that they   examine observe
[9]................. in tiny hooks which [10]................. entangled in the fabric. The idea of   cover become
Velcro [11]................. .   born

Velcro might never [12]................. it on to the market without the skills of a   make
French weaver. First attempts to make the locking tape from cotton [13].................   run
into problems when mass production [14]................. . The breakthrough [15].................   attempt come
when de Mestral discovered that if nylon [16]................. under infrared light near-   sew
indestructible hooks [17]................. . The final product [18]................. of two strips of   create make
nylon, one with thousands of hooks, the other with thousands of loops.

Velcro [19]................. to the general public's attention when it began to   come
[20]................. as a quick fastening for shoes and clothing. Today Velcro [21].................   use use
everywhere, for functions ranging from keeping car-seat covers in position to
preventing equipment floating about in US space shuttles.

The ultimate test for the Velcro enthusiast is "bar fly jumping". After dressing up
in a Velcro-coated suit, the fan [22]................. himself at a Velcro-coated wall. If the   throw
Velcro is up to strength, he or she [23]................. stuck to the wall. If not, he [2]   get
[4]................. to the floor. There is no room for cheap imitations.   plunge

15.4 Opposites WORD STUDY

A Write down the opposites of these adjectives.

easy ...difficult... accurate .... confident ....

quiet .... fresh (bread) .... empty ....

polite .... safe .... expensive ....

B And write down the opposites of these verbs.

tell the truth .... turn on .... support ....

find .... succeed .... finish ....

win .... reject .... break, damage ....

15.5 Paper 4: Listening – Parts 1 and 2   EXAM TECHNIQUES

 A

Always read the questions through carefully before the first playing of the recording starts. In Part I you'll hear the questions in the recording as well as seeing them on the Question paper. In Part 2 look to see what information you've got to listen out for.

📟 **You will hear people talking in eight different situations. For Questions 1–8, choose the best answer, A, B or C.**

1 Listen to two people talking. What are they looking at?
    A a bicycle   **B** a car   **C** a motorbike   **1**

2 Two people are talking. What has the man just bought?
    A a remote control   **B** a video recorder   **C** a television   **2**

3 Listen to a woman talking on the phone. Who is she talking to?
    A a repair man   **B** a friend   **C** someone in an office   **3**

4 You're at a railway station. What are the two people talking about?
    A a ticket machine   **B** a drinks machine   **C** a chocolate machine   **4**

5 A man is talking about returning something to a shop. How does he feel?
    A furious   **B** amused   **C** disappointed   **5**

6 You hear two people talking about computers. Which of them is going to buy one?
    A the man   **B** both of them   **C** neither of them   **6**

7 Listen to a man speaking. Who is he?
    A a scientist   **B** shop assistant   **C** a museum guide   **7**

8 Listen to two people talking. How does the woman feel?
    A worried   **B** disappointed   **C** pleased   **8**

B

📟 **You'll hear part of a radio programme. For Questions 9–18 fill in the missing information.**

ARPANET (1966) was intended to work
even if the network was partially destroyed by a ⬚ **9**

ARPANET was based on two principles: ⬚ **10**

there was no ⬚ **11**

it connected computers of different ⬚ **12**

Internet Protocol (1983) controls the way
that data to be transmitted is split into ⬚ **13**

Individual users of a network are known as ⬚ **14**

Individual messages are first sent to computer called a ⬚ **15**

Data is sent between networks by computers called ⬚ **16**

The World Wide Web (1989) was created by CERN,
based in ⬚ **17**

The first web browser became available in ⬚ **18**

When are connections slowest on the Internet? ⬚ **19**

15.6 Prepositions   REVISION

This exercise revises some of the Prepositions from 11.5, 12.5, 13.6 and 14.5 in the Student's Book.

Fill each gap with one word.

1 It's a secret: I'm telling you this in ....

2 It was such a sad story that we were all in ....

3 She .... for being late.

4 Salt .... of sodium and chloride.

5 I'm .... on you to help me.

6 If you spend enough time .... for the exam, you should do well.

7 Although he was .... from a bad headache he went out for the evening.

8 How much did you .... for the tickets?

9 I'm getting very .... of this cold, wet weather.

10 She .... on helping me, even though I was perfectly .... of doing it by myself.

11 .... on your engagement!

12 After a long climb the mountaineers .... in reaching the summit.

15.7 What can go wrong?   SPEAKING AND WRITING

If possible, arrange to do **B** with another student. If this isn't possible, record your answers to the questions using a cassette recorder and a microphone.

 A Look at the things in the picture and decide what you could say if you are asked:

Look at these gadgets and tools. Decide which of them you think people find most useful and why. Which of them could you happily do without? What can go wrong with them and how can you fix them?

B Working with another student, talk about the gadgets and tools.

or Working alone, talk about the gadgets using a cassette recorder and a microphone. Then listen to the recording and try to improve your answers.

or Speaking quietly to yourself, give your answers to each of the questions.

When you've finished writing, make sure you check your work.

C One of the video recorders in your college has broken down. The principal has asked you to write a report on what is wrong with it, which will be sent with the VCR to the repair workshop. Write your report (120–180 words).

Count the number of words you've written. Then compare your report with the Model report on page 105.

In particular, look for mistakes in:
*Spelling
Prepositions Verb forms and endings
Articles*

Keeping up to date

16.1 / In the news   VOCABULARY

There are 24 words connected with the news, crime and politics hidden in this puzzle. Circle each one you can find.

```
n e w s e d i t o r i a l
b e h e a d l i n e o r w
r e p o r t m u r d e r a
e c a r t o o n j a i l r
p i g d i s a s t e r p o
o r d o c u m e n t a r y
r e c o l u m n a s s e a
t g o v e r n m e n t s c
e r o b b e r y t c o i p
r a t l e a d e r r r d h
e l e c t i o n i i y e o
s i d p a r l i a m e n t
r e f u g e e s l e o t o
```

16.2 / The past – 3: Reported speech   GRAMMAR

If you choose to write a story in Part 2 of the Writing paper (Paper 2), try to use both direct and indirect speech. Direct speech is usually easier to get right, but make sure you put each different speaker on a new line and use inverted commas correctly.

Complete the second sentence so that it has a similar meaning to the first sentence, using the word in bold. Use between two and five words, including the word given. Don't change the word given.

1 "Please help me," she said.

   asked   She .... her.

2 "I can't do this without your help," he said to us.

   claimed   He .... do it on his own.

3 "It's true. I did commit the crime," he said.

   committed   He admitted .... the crime.

4 "You should check your work before you hand it in," she said to me.

   advised   She .... work before handing it in.

5 "Are you feeling all right?" she said to me.

   asked   She .... feeling OK .

6 "Why are you writing in pencil?" he asked me.

   using   He wondered why .... a pen.

7 "What time does the film begin?" she asked me.

   when   She wanted to ....

8 "What are you doing today?" he said to me on Friday.

   doing   He asked me what I ....

9 "I'll come when I've finished my work," he said.

   when   He promised that he .... finished his work.

10 "Phone him tomorrow," she said to me on Saturday.

   ring   She told me ....

16.3 Paper 1: Reading – Part 4 EXAM TECHNIQUES

 Look at 16.8 **A** on page 134 in the Student's Book. Make sure that you know what to expect in each part of the Reading paper.

B This exercise is similar to the one you'll have to do in Part 4 of the Reading paper. Try to complete it in 15–20 minutes.

You are going to read about four burglars. For Questions 1–14, choose from the burglars (A–D).

Which burglar …

was sorry for causing distress to his/her victims? `1` ☐

woke up the family's pet? `2` ☐

broke into buildings which were unoccupied? `3` ☐

claimed that the family had asked him/her to stay with them? `4` ☐

made legal history? `5` ☐

had a partner in crime? `6` ☐

had been seen by neighbours before the family knew he/she was in the house? `7` ☐

had had too much to drink? `8` ☐

stole the most valuable things? `9` ☐

tried to give a false name to the police? `10` ☐

was arrested at the scene of the crime? `11` ☐

was female? `12` ☐

was free for the longest time before being caught? `13` ☐

woke up the eldest son of the family? `14` ☐

> In Part 4 of the Reading paper (Paper 1), the questions are not in the same order as the information in the texts. Read the questions through first before you read the texts. Then look through the texts to find the answers to the questions. You don't need to understand every word of the texts – don't worry about unfamiliar words.

> There are about 14 questions in Part 4 of the Reading paper, each worth one mark. But the questions in Parts 1–3 are each worth two marks. Part 4 tests how well you can locate information in the text(s).

A

A BURGLAR who listened at windows and doors to see if properties were empty before breaking in was jailed for a year yesterday after being caught by ear prints left at the scenes of his crimes.

Calvin Sewell, 25, a known burglar, left ear prints at 13 different properties in south London, and became the first criminal to be prosecuted on the evidence of his ears alone.

An expert in facial mapping came up with a perfect match to the prints the court was told.

Prof Peter Vanezis, from the University of Glasgow, who is also a forensic pathologist, worked with the Metropolitan Police on the unusual case. Afterwards, Prof Vanezis said: "Ear prints are as unique as fingerprints. From the age of four months we all have different ears.

"No two identical twins have the same ears and even the ears on each side of your head are unique," he added. The prints were usually left when a suspect leaned against a door, window or wall, and were collected by police at the scene in the same way as fingerprints, he said.

A mould was made of the prints in this case, which were matched to Sewell. He pleaded guilty to five charges of burglary.

The investigating police officer, Detective Constable Alan Hodgson, said he had been so impressed by the ear-printing technique that he was going to encourage fellow officers to keep an eye out for ear prints during future investigations.

B

A BURGLAR who fell asleep on a child's bed while stealing a video recorder from a family's home has been jailed for four years.

Tony Pratt, 22, lapsed into such a deep sleep that two police doghandlers had trouble waking him when they arrived at the house. He had unplugged the recorder ready to carry it away when he slumped on to the bed, waking Craig Richardson, 13, who was beneath the covers.

Craig managed to slide out and tiptoe into his mother's room to tell her to telephone the police, Newcastle upon Tyne Crown Court heard.

John Evans, prosecuting, said: "This is a somewhat bizarre case. It was clear to everyone that Pratt was heavily intoxicated. The police eventually arrived and had some trouble waking Pratt up. When he came round he tried to tell them he was someone else."

Pratt, of Newcastle, admitted burglary and the court heard he had carried out two other raids on homes and had eight previous convictions for similar offences.

John Aitken, defending, said: "Pratt was heavily intoxicated that night and was more likely to fall asleep than anything else. He offered no resistance when arrested and didn't get away with a thing."

Sentencing him, Judge Jim Stephenson said: "Households in this city must be protected from the likes of you."

Craig's mother Eleanor Richardson, 38, said yesterday that the family had lived in the house on the Scotswood estate, Newcastle, for the past six years but were considering moving as a result of the burglary. Her husband John, 54, is a seaman and they have two other children, Samantha, 15, and Jordan, 3.

Mrs Richardson said: "Craig woke up to say someone was on his bed. We went downstairs to phone the police but they were already outside. Someone must have seen Pratt breaking in and called them first.

"They had a right job waking him up. He was out cold. When they got him awake I started shouting at him, asking him what he was doing in my house. The cheeky man had the nerve to claim he had been invited. He got in through the kitchen window and was cut to bits. He was so stupid. I have not come across anyone as daft before. He really is a prat and lives up to his name."

C

MOPSY, a rabbit with the ability to thump its foot at a very high decibel level, foiled a burglary at its owners' home by waking the household.

A judge was told that the animal drummed so loudly that it woke its owners and the woman thief and an accomplice were seen making their getaway on stolen mountain bikes.

Robert Jenkins, 46, his wife, Anne and their three children, Abigail, 16, Sam, 14 and 12-year-old Daniel, were asleep at their home in Leatherhead, Surrey, last June when the noise started at 3am. Police arrested Louise Hazeltine, 23, shortly after.

It led to her appearing before Guildford Crown Court on two charges of burglary and two separate counts of theft.

After hearing that Hazeltine was six months' pregnant, Judge Keith Bassingthwaite imposed a two-year probation order on each charge to run concurrently.

D

A BURGLAR who was wanted by the police for three years was caught when his own home was broken into, a court was told yesterday.

John Michell had his fingerprints taken for elimination purposes, Norwich Crown Court was told, and police then discovered that he was a wanted man in Norfolk. Michell, 31, unemployed, of Bedford, admitted burglary in April at the home of the Rev Edwin Softley of Ten Mile Bank, near King's Lynn, Norfolk, and stealing items valued at more than £2,000, including a Communion cross and four silver chalices. He also admitted attempted burglary in May, stealing petrol from a garage, damaging a telephone box and driving while disqualified.

Michell was jailed for 12 months and banned from driving for two years. The court was told that Michell had previous convictions for burglary. Richard Potts, defending, said Michell now realised the seriousness of the offences. Since his own home was burgled, he realised the pain it caused to others.

 Look at 16.8 **B** on page 134 in the Student's Book. Do a complete practice test for Paper 1 and time yourself. If you take longer than 75 minutes, you'll need to improve your speed. If you have time in hand, make sure you check all your answers at the end.

Paper 4: Listening – Parts 3 and 4

A

 You will hear five people talking about crimes. For Questions 19–23, choose from the list A–F what each speaker says. Use the letters only once. There is one extra letter which you do not need to use.

A The criminal ran into the arms of the police.	Speaker 1	☐ **19**
B The criminal was caught because he looked very funny.	Speaker 2	☐ **20**
C The criminal was arrested three months after the crime.	Speaker 3	☐ **21**
D The criminal hasn't been caught.	Speaker 4	☐ **22**
E The police arrested the criminal the next day.	Speaker 5	☐ **23**
F The police knew the name of the criminal.		

> Part 3 of the Listening paper (Paper 4) consists of interviews with five people. You have to decide who said what. Listen carefully because something one speaker says may only be slightly different from what another one says.

B

You will hear part of a radio interview about an unusual transatlantic crossing. For Questions 24–30 choose the best answer, A, B or C.

> Part 4 of the Listening paper is usually an interview or radio programme, but there may be different kinds of questions:
> • Multiple-choice questions, as here.
> • Questions where you have to decide which of two speakers said what – or whether neither did. You have to write A (or the first speaker's initial), B (or the second speaker's initial) or N for Neither in the boxes.
> • True or false questions. You have to write T for True or F for False in the boxes.

24 How long did the journey take?
   A 25 days   **B** 36 days   **C** 63 days
   ☐ **24**

25 Where did they hope to land in Europe?
   A England   **B** France   **C** Ireland
   ☐ **25**

26 How many people were on board the 'The Son of Town Hall'?
   A three   **B** four   **C** five
   ☐ **26**

27 How many dogs were on board the ship?
   A one   **B** two   **C** three
   ☐ **27**

28 Who ate pasta during the voyage?
   A the dogs   **B** the people   **C** the dogs and the people
   ☐ **28**

29 How long did they expect the journey to take?
   A 13 days   **B** 30 days   **C** 60 days
   ☐ **29**

30 How long will they stay in Ireland?
   A two weeks   **B** six weeks   **C** six months
   ☐ **30**

16.5 **Good news or bad news?** SPEAKING

If possible, arrange to do **B** with another student. If this isn't possible, record your answers to the questions using a cassette recorder and a microphone.

A **Look at these questions and think how you can reply to them.**

In Part 4 of the Speaking paper (Paper 5) the examiner will ask you some questions about a topic. You'll have to discuss these questions with the other candidate.

- How do you find out about what's in the news?
- Do you think it's important to know what's going on in the world? Why?
- Do you prefer to watch the news on TV, listen to the radio or read a paper? Why?
- How do the people you know keep up to date with the news?
- What kind of news items do you find most interesting? Why?
- What do you think life would be like without television, radio and newspapers?

B **Working with another student, discuss the questions.**

or Working alone, record your answers to the questions using a cassette recorder and a microphone. Then listen to the recording and try to improve your answers.

or Speaking quietly to yourself, give your answers to each of the questions.

16.6 **A letter to the editor** WRITING

A You've read this article in a newspaper and made the notes on the right. Write a letter to the editor of the newpaper explaining your views on the topic.

Good news!

More good news in your *Daily Bugle* next week

From Monday this newspaper will be different and better! Here are some of the changes you can look forward to:

- Although we will cover all the important news from around the world, we promise that when good things happen you will read about them in the *Daily Bugle*.

- The main story on the front page will always be good news, not bad news.

- Expanded sports coverage. Six full pages of sports every day.

- A new Review page. But instead of criticising films, books and arts events our reviewers will describe them – but let you make your own mind up.

- A new Editorial section. There will be two editorials about each event, giving both points of view.

- A new cartoon page with the funniest cartoons to keep you smiling throughout the day and Jokes of the Day to make you laugh.

The new "Good News" Bugle. THE paper for the 21st Century.

(handwritten notes:)
What do you mean by good news?

The most important event should be the main story.
There is already too much sport.

Reviews help me to find out what films to see and what books to read.

With most events there are more than just two points of view.

Yes! Great idea.

B Write a letter to the editor of the *Daily Bugle* (120–180 words). Then compare your letter with the Model letter on page 106.

17 It's a small world

Countries, cities and nationalities VOCABULARY

What nationality is someone from each of these cities? Add the nationality words to the puzzle on the right. (Make sure your spelling was correct when you check your answers later!)

1 Oslo
2 Warsaw
3 Athens
4 Rome
5 Beijing
6 São Paulo
7 Montreal
8 Stockholm
9 Geneva
10 Lisbon
11 Istanbul
12 Cairo
13 Madrid
14 Tokyo
15 Munich
16 Buenos Aires
17 Dublin
18 Brussels
19 Amsterdam
20 Sydney
21 (down) These two continents are joined together. (4 words)

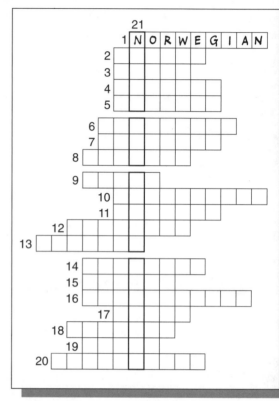

17.2 **Paper 1: Reading – Part 3** EXAM TECHNIQUES

 A Look at this advice:

> **Golden rules for Part 3**
>
> Read the sentence *before* and the sentence *after* each gap very carefully. That's where you'll probably find the words or ideas that connect with the missing sentence.
>
> Words to look for in the missing sentences *and* in the sentence before and after each gap:
>
> 1 *This* – Look for the idea that this refers to.
> 2 Pronouns: *it he she they* – Look for the person or thing they refer to.
> 3 Time words: *then later after that when again* – Look for the event mentioned before.
> 4 Place words: *there here away back* – Look for the place mentioned before.
> 5 Conjunctions: *also so therefore however but* – Look for the connected or contrasted idea.

B You're going to read an article by a woman who spent six months travelling around the world. Eight sentences have been removed from the article. Choose from the sentences (A–J) the ones which fit in each gap (1–8). There is one extra sentence which you don't need to use. There is an example at the beginning (0).

First read the article quickly through, then read the sentences. Cross out the example sentence so that it doesn't distract you. Then read the article again and try to fit in the easier sentences, and cross them out one by one. Then look again at the sentences that are still left and decide where they can fit. If you don't know, guess! If you have two left and one gap to fill, you have a 50/50 chance of guessing right.

Back to the past

Emily Barr tries to pick up the threads of her old life

"Ladies and gentlemen," says the captain's voice, "We are now beginning our descent into Heathrow, although you can't see it through the cloud. The outside temperature is 10 degrees. Welcome to Britain."

I get out the blanket which everyone in Pakistan wraps around them when warmth is needed, and which has become something of a security blanket, and swathe myself in it. **0** **D**

On the drive back to Bristol, I look out of the window at how clean and tidy everything is, and marvel at the way everyone keeps to the correct side of the road, while nobody swings blithely around blind corners trusting god to keep them safe. **1** Everything is orderly. **2** It's packaged, sanitised, unrecognisable, a billion miles and years away from the street stalls of India and Pakistan. Even though I don't eat meat, I would rather see it laid out in all its glory as in Asia – a severed head on the counter, four feet standing next to a bloody carcass.

After a few days of hanging out with the family in Bristol, walking in the sudden sunshine and handing over all my money to the photo shop in exchange for 432 photos, I decide it's time to go to London. **3** Maybe I will again. But I feel that I want to hide. When I get on the Tube with the rucksack which is still my mobile home, people look at me quickly and turn away, dismissively. Perhaps they think I'm an Australian backpacker.

After the first of several nights meeting up with old, dear friends, I realise I was wrong to assume I wouldn't get ill here. You do have days of lying in bed groaning and weakly sipping a glass of water. In Asia it's probably fever; in London it's a hangover. After weeks in a Muslim country, my alcohol tolerance is low indeed.

I struggle bravely onwards, and go one night to meet some journalists and television people. **4** I've forgotten how to speak small talk. I soon discover that I don't want to live in London any more.

Everyone asks "How was it?" Then they say, "You're not as brown as I thought you'd be," and, finally, comes the dreaded question: "What are you going to do now?" **5** I am not, for instance, going to work in an office.

So how was it, really, the year that already seems like a dream? Thirteen countries. Two romances – one of them lasting. **6** The biggest country in the world. One election. Three wars. One tattoo. Three haircuts. Mount Everest. One Muslim, three Communist, three Buddhist, and three western countries. One near armed robbery. Extensive wine research in three countries. Serious trekking in two. One six-month period of unbroken happiness. A hundred thousand previously unimagined experiences and different perspectives. **7** The realisation that anyone can really do anything if they put their mind to it. New reserves of confidence. Horror at the insecurities that used to plague me. A host of possibilities. **8**

In Part 3 of the Reading paper (Paper 3) there may be 6 or 7 missing bits (plus an example). The missing bits may be sentences or they may be short paragraphs.

A A year to remember.

B At the moment I can only answer this question in negatives.

C Later, in a supermarket, I feel that I am in a dream.

D My blanket and I will face this together.

E Most of my friends live there, and I used to.

F Surprises at every turn.

G I am happy to be home at last.

H The highest country in the world.

I The sky is grey and the roads are grey, and there is none of the distinctive smell that makes Asia what it is.

J But I don't know what to say.

17.3 Comparing and contrasting   GRAMMAR REVIEW

In Part 3 of the Use of English paper (Paper 3) you have to write your answers in the spaces on the Answer sheet, not the Question paper. You should write in pen, not pencil. But if you're not quite sure of a sentence, you can pencil in your first idea on the Question paper and later write it again neatly in the space on the Answer sheet. Your spelling must be 100% correct.

Complete the second sentence so that it has a similar meaning to the first sentence, using the word in bold. Use between two and five words, including the word given. Don't change the word given.

1 There are fewer people in France than in Germany.

inhabitants   France doesn't have .... Germany.

2 There are no countries larger than Brazil in South America.

bigger   Brazil .... all the countries in South America.

3 Argentina is also large, but not as large as Brazil.

second   Argentina .... in South America.

4 There are more mountains in Greece than in Britain.

has   Britain .... Greece.

5 The population of Japan is half that of the USA.

twice   In the USA there are .... there are in Japan.

6 Russia is twice as big as Canada.

size   Canada .... Russia.

7 There are more mountains in Japan than in Germany.

mountainous   Germany .... Japan.

8 There is less rainforest in Peru than in Brazil.

rainforest   In Peru there is not .... there is in Brazil.

9 There's not much difference in climate between Spain and Greece.

similar   The Spanish climate .... the Greek climate.

10 Norwich is far safer than Miami.

much   Miami .... Norwich.

17.4 Paper 3: Use of English – Part 5 Word formation
EXAM TECHNIQUES

A Read this advice first:

In Part 5 of the Use of English paper there are ten questions (plus one example). You may have to add a prefix and/or a suffix, form a compound word or change the spelling:

strong → strength   strengthen

day → daily   daylight   daytime

honest → dishonest   honesty   dishonesty   honestly   dishonestly

rain → rainy   raindrop   raindrops   rainbow

sun → sunny   sunshine   sunlight

B Read the text below. Use the word given in capitals at the end of each line to form a word that fits in the space in the same line.

In Part 5 of the Use of English paper make sure the word you write fits in the context correctly – and that your spelling is 100% correct. Don't forget to make a noun plural if the context demands it.

TRAVELLING ABROAD

One of the greatest **(0)** ..pleasures.. of travelling abroad is   PLEASE
experiencing the **(1)** .... differences between my country   CULTURE
and other countries. **(2)** .... , it must be said that the vast   FORTUNE
(3) .... of holiday brochures focus on sunshine, sea and sand.   MAJOR
But for me it is the local **(4)** .... who are the main   INHABIT
(5) .... in any foreign country – not sunbathing on a   ATTRACT
sandy beach at the **(6)** ....   SEA

But before you travel you have to make **(7)** .... for the trip. This   PREPARE
has to be done **(8)** .... by reading about the places you're going to   THOROUGH
visit. **(9)** .... , there's no substitute for a good guidebook as a way   SURPRISE
to gain this kind of **(10)** ....   KNOW

17.5 Local customs   LISTENING

🔲 Listen to five people talking about their experiences in foreign countries. Choose from the list A–F what each speaker says about their experiences. Use the letters only once. There is one extra letter which you do not need to use.

In Part 3 of the Listening paper (Paper 4) read all the alternatives very carefully. The odd one out is likely to be only slightly wrong and some of the correct ones may be only slightly different.

A This person felt embarrassed.

B This person was hungry in the afternoon.

C The local people thought this person was being unfriendly.

D This person was hungry after dinner.

E This person got into trouble with one of the local people.

F This person never got used to the eating habits.

Speaker 1 ☐ **1**

Speaker 2 ☐ **2**

Speaker 3 ☐ **3**

Speaker 4 ☐ **4**

Speaker 5 ☐ **5**

17.6 Comparing and contrasting   SPEAKING

If possible, arrange to do this with another student. If this isn't possible, record your answers to the questions using a cassette recorder and a microphone.

 A Look at the two photos and think what you can say about them.

In Part 2 of the Speaking paper (Paper 5), listen carefully to what the other candidate says – you'll have to comment on this when he or she has spoken for a minute.

B Working with another student, talk for one minute about the photos. How do you think life is different for the people in each place?

or Working alone, record your one-minute talk. Then listen to the recording and try to improve your answers.

or Speaking quietly to yourself, speak about the photos for one minute.

17.7 **Paper 2: Writing – Part 2**   EXAM TECHNIQUES

A Read this information about Part 2 of the Writing paper.

> If you haven't read a Background reading text, you have to choose one of three tasks in Part 2. There will be three of these task types:
>
> An **article** for a newspaper or magazine whose readers are your own age or share your interests. The purpose of the article is to interest the readers and probably include your opinions or comments.
>
> An **informal letter** written to someone you know, such as a pen-friend. The purpose of the letter is to interest the reader and you'll probably be sharing your experiences, or explaining your feelings or opinions.
>
> (If the letter in Part 1 is an informal letter, there might be a **formal letter** in Part 2.)
>
> A **letter of application** for a job or scholarship. The purpose of the letter is to get the job or the scholarship.
>
> A **report** written for your boss or teacher or for fellow-students or colleagues. The purpose of the report is to give facts and usually your suggestions or recommendations.
>
> A discursive **composition** or essay, usually written for a teacher. The purpose is to give your opinions and/or suggestions on a topic.
>
> A **short story** for a magazine or to enter a competition. The purpose of the story is to interest the readers, who are people of your own age (and get paid by the magazine or win first prize).

B And look at these *Golden rules.*

> **Golden rules for Part 2**
>
> 1 Read the instructions for each Question very carefully. Twice. Spend several minutes deciding which to do unless, for example, you're good at writing stories and there is a story-writing task.
>
> 2 Follow the instructions exactly. If you don't quite understand the instructions for one of the Questions, don't do it.
>
> 3 Make notes before you start writing. Re-read the instructions to make sure the points you've noted are relevant.
>
> 4 When you've finished writing, check your work for mistakes and slips of the pen.

C Write an answer to one of the Questions 2–4 in this part. Write your answer in 120–180 words in an appropriate style.

What about style? The safest thing to do is to use a not-too-formal, not-too-informal style. Don't try to write in a style you feel uncomfortable with.

> 2 A magazine you read is going to publish a special issue on the pros and cons of world travel. Write an article for the magazine giving your views and describing some of your experiences.
>
>   Write your **article**.
>
> 3 You have decided to enter a short story competition. The composition must begin or end with these words:
>
>   It's a small world
>
>   Write your **story** for the competition.

In the exam, don't forget to put the number of the Question in the box.

> 4 The local tourist information office has asked you to report on what tourists from abroad like and dislike about your town or city and how their experience could be improved.
>
>   Write your **report**.

D Compare your answer with the Model answers on page 106.

And remember: you don't have to tell the truth in the exam.

Yes, but is it art?

18.1 Art and music VOCABULARY

There are 26 words connected with
art and music hidden in this puzzle.
Circle each one you can find.

```
a m s d r a m a t i s t l
r y c o m p o s e r i h a
t v u z a b a g c i n e n
s o l o d a c t o n g a d
u p p a i n t i n g e t s
r e t p j d o l d a r r c
r r u i a i r l u b a e a
e a r a z o r p c s v a p
a b e n z i p o t t e r e
l v i o l i n p o r o c k
i o r c h e s t r a v e l
s t a g e n i u s c e l o
t v p o r t r a i t r l o
```

18.2 The future GRAMMAR REVIEW

Read through the
whole of the
Grammar
reference section
in the Student's
Book (pages
170–185) before
the exam.

Complete the second sentence so that it has a similar meaning to the first sentence, using the
word in bold. Use between two and five words, including the word given. Don't change the
word given.

1 Your train will arrive at 10 o'clock. I'll be waiting on the platform.

   train I'll be waiting on the platform at 10 o'clock when ....

2 We must get to the gallery before it closes at 6 o'clock.

   already If we get to the gallery after 6 o'clock it ....

3 My sister-in-law's child is due in September.

   have My brother's .... a baby in September.

4 I have arranged to meet my friend at the station on Saturday.

   pick I .... at the station on Saturday.

5 What is the best time for us to meet?

   get When .... together?

6 I'm going to be so late that I won't get there before the end of the lesson.

   arrive By the time I .... over.

7 I'm going to study. What are you going to do?

   while What will you .... studying?

8 I'm going to pay you a visit, when would be a good time?

   round When .... to visit you?

9 I don't expect to start working till 9 o'clock.

   begin I .... before 9 o'clock.

10 After the exam it's time for me to have a holiday.

    on I .... when the exam is over.

A

First read this information and advice about Part 1.

> Part 1 of the Reading Paper tests whether you can identify the main ideas or main points of each paragraph.
>
> There are 6 or 7 questions (plus an example). Each question is worth two marks.
>
> You may have to match either headings or summary sentences to the paragraphs in the text.
>
> Read the summary sentences or headings first, then look at the text.
>
> Be ready to change your mind if you discover that one of the headings goes better with a later paragraph.
>
> Don't leave any blanks – guess if necessary.

B

What if I make a mistake with the first answer? Won't that mean that all the other answers will be wrong? The texts and questions in every exam are carefully chosen and thoroughly pre-tested to make sure this can't happen. (This also applies to Part 3.)

Look at this newspaper article and choose the most suitable heading from the list A–J for each paragraph (1–8) in the article. There's one extra heading which you don't need to use. The headline is given as an example (0).

A   A dissatisfied sponsor

B   An art show with no paintings

C   Comments from two of the students

D   Fellow students impressed by the show

E   Reactions from the union

F   Reactions from the university

G   Students make an exhibition of themselves

H   Supporters dissatisfied

I   The climax of the show

J   The purpose of the stunt

0   G

THIRTEEN art students given a grant and sponsorship of £1,600 to put on an exhibition spent the money on a week's holiday on the Costa del Sol and returned home claiming that the trip was conceptual art.

1

Two sponsors, including the Leeds University students' union, which gave a grant of £1,126, said yesterday that they had been misled by the students. They claimed that the stunt gave art a bad name and demanded their money back.

2

But the 13 students, the entire third year on Leeds University's Fine Art course, said their holiday – when they swam, sunbathed and visited nightclubs – was designed "to challenge people's perception of art" and to make people discuss whether there was any limit to what could be described as art.

3

One of the students, Matt Dunning, 22, said: "It was essential for us to go to the Costa del Sol because that created controversy." A fellow participant, Emma Robertson, said: "This is leisure as art. It is art and it was an exhibition. People have very fixed ideas about what art is and we are interested in the media reaction because we want people to discuss what art is."

4

About 60 lecturers, local artists and fellow students invited to the first-night party for the exhibition – enigmatically titled Going Places – were surprised when they entered a gallery empty except for a large bowl of sangria, the sound of flamenco music and a drama student dressed as an air hostess.

5

As they stood around, uncertain what would happen next, they were led to a double-decker bus, driven to Leeds-Bradford airport and left in a bar overlooking the arrivals area. A short time later, they saw the entire group of laughing, sun-tanned, third-year students – who had used the money to buy £185 flight-and-accommodation packages – march through Customs armed with souvenirs from the Costa del Sol. The two groups met, the stunt was explained and they all went to the bar again, running up a bill of £180. They spent a couple of hours discussing the meaning of art before they were bussed back to Leeds city centre.

6

The Students' Union, which said it had been led to believe that the art students were mounting a more traditional exhibition and that the grant of £1,126 was for framing, materials and hiring a gallery, suffered a serious humour failure yesterday. Ruth Wilkin, the union's communications officer, said: "We have asked for the money back. When we gave the money there was no mention of any holidays. We have very limited resources and we are trying to raise £20,000 for a minibus for the disabled. It is fairly outrageous and pretty upsetting to see some of our students taking money for a holiday when it should have been spent on a much worthier cause."

7

Myles Dutton, who runs the Dixon Bate art shop in Leeds, was one of several commercial sponsors who gave more than £400 for what they thought was a conventional exhibition. He said: "I gave £50. It's not a lot but I feel I have been tricked and I want my money back."

8

A university spokesman declined to condemn the students and said: "It should be noted that on little more than £1,000 they managed to spend a week in Spain, hire a space for the exhibition, hire the double-decker bus and pay for the drinks at the bar at the airport. They got a lot out of it."

18.4 The next day ...   LISTENING

This is the last Listening exercise. You'll probably do Paper 4 a few weeks before Papers 1–3, during the same week as Paper 5. Good luck!

You'll hear more about the art students' holiday trip. Complete the sentences which summarise what the reporter says.

The number of students involved was _____ **1**

The beach photos were taken in Scarborough, a _____ **2** near Leeds.

They got their suntans from _____ **3**

The students were allowed to arrive through _____ **4** at the airport.

The Airport authorities announced a fake flight on the _____ **5**

The students told the Airport authorities they were making a _____ **6**

The Students' Union still wants _____ **7**

The students say that their stunt _____ **8** the boundaries of art.

18.5 Paper 2: Writing – Part 1   EXAM TECHNIQUES

 A Read this information about Part 1 of the Writing paper.

Paper 2 Part 1

You must answer Question 1. The letter you have to write may be formal or informal. You may have to do some of these things:

say what action you intend to take	ask the other person to take action
give information	request information
make complaints or corrections	make suggestions
ask for feedback	

The input text may be an advertisement, a letter, a postcard, a diary or a short article. There will be notes of points to include or questions to ask. There may be pictures or diagrams to look at.

 B And here are some *Dos* and *Don'ts*.

---

1 Consider Part 2 first. If there's a question there you can do easily, it will put you in a good mood for doing Part 1.
2 Read the instructions and the input texts carefully. Twice.
3 Make notes on the Question paper. Use a highlighter to mark the information you must include or questions you must ask.
4 You must cover all the essential points. Check your notes before you start writing.
5 Don't write any addresses.
6 Try not to quote word for word from the input text.
7 Use key words from the input text, but try to rephrase some of the information in other words.
8 Don't just write a list of questions or statements.
9 Look carefully to see if you have to add a piece of information, or a suggestion or request of your own. But don't include any irrelevant information.
10 Part 1 and Part 2 are both worth the same number of marks, so don't spend too long on Part 1. Make sure you have enough time to do Part 2.

18.6 An exhibition   SPEAKING AND WRITING

A Working with a partner, or alone, say what you think about this picture. What do you like and dislike about it? Is it art, do you think?

This is the last Speaking exercise. You'll probably do Paper 5 a few weeks before Papers 1–3, during the same week as Paper 4. Good luck!

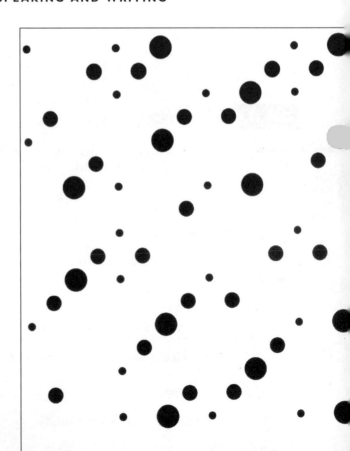

B

Spend no more than 45 minutes on this task, including the time it takes to read the instructions and check your work afterwards.

It may not be easy work up any enthusiasm for this kind of task, where you have to imagine a suitable reader. Before the exam, try to think of an imaginary English pen-friend to have in your mind for this kind of task.

1 It is July 1st. You saw an advertisement for this exhibition of works by an artist your friend Bob adores. Bob lives in Newcastle – a long way from London, where you live.

Read the advertisement, train information and your notes carefully. Then write a letter to your friend, giving the necessary information about the exhibition and trying to persuade him to come to London to visit the exhibition with you.

Write a **letter** of between **120** and **180** words in an appropriate style. Do not write any addresses.

Bridget Riley
Bob's favourite artist

Paintings from the 1960s and 70s

Bridget Riley is one of the most celebrated figures of contemporary painting. This major new exhibition, organised by the Serpentine Gallery in close collaboration with the artist, brings together over thirty paintings created during the 1960s and 70s.

Serpentine Gallery, Kensington Gardens, London W2 3XA

19 June–30 August

Admission free NB!!   Open daily 10am–6pm

GNER	Saturdays			
Newcastle	0700	0730	0800	0831
London (King's Cross)	1009	1038	1109	1140
London (King's Cross)	1800	1840	1900	2030
Newcastle	2102	2151	2215	2347

best train

best train

Saturdays in July only:
Day return including free London Transport Travelcard: £39
Tickets must be purchased at least 7 days before travel.

less than half price
NB must book

Meet you at King's Cross — need to know which train to meet
Have lunch together — chance to spend day together

C

Compare your letter with the Model letter on page 107.

19 Other people

Personality and behaviour VOCABULARY

All the clues are adjectives you can use to describe someone.

How can you describe someone who …

1 falls in love easily?
2 behaves badly – especially children?
3 gets upset if someone talks to his/her boyfriend/girlfriend?
4 you can trust?
5 is liked by most people?
6 gets upset easily?
7 gets angry easily?
8 is a true friend?
9 doesn't think about other people?
10 usually seems happy?
11 is kind?
12 has a good sense of humour and tells jokes?
13 studies and works hard?
14 gives other people gifts?
15 is sure of himself/herself?
16 feels embarrassed when meeting new people?
17 (down) If you get on really well with someone you can say "We're … … … … ." (4 words)

[Crossword grid with 1 across answer: R O M A N T I C]

19.2 **Paper 1: Reading – Part 2** EXAM TECHNIQUES

A First read this information and advice about Part 2.

> Part 2 of the Reading paper mainly tests detailed understanding of the text.
> There are 7 or 8 multiple-choice questions, each worth two marks.
> The questions are in the same order as the order of information in the text.
> Other questions that might be asked:
> "What might a suitable title for the text be?"
> "What does the writer mean by *X* in line Y?" – you have to work out the meaning from the context.
> "What does the word *it* refer to in line Y?" – you have to say what a pronoun refers to.

B Read this article about left-handed people. For Questions 1–8, choose the answer (A, B, C or D) which you think fits best according to the text.

1 What is a suitable title for this text?

   A How left-handers cope in offices **B** Left-handed people are strange
   C Don't be unkind to left-handers **D** The advantages of being left-handed

2 How did left-handers used to be treated at school?

   A Like everyone else. **B** They were punished for being left-handed.
   C They were laughed at. **D** They were pitied.

3 Why do left-handed workers have more accidents than right-handed workers?

   A They are unlucky. **B** They are clumsy.
   C Equipment is designed for right-handers. **D** Offices must be rearranged for left-handers.

4 What does Nikki Behar mean by *them* in line 38?

   A desks **B** drawers **C** letters **D** envelopes

5 Where is the best place to put your phone on your desk?

   A On the left. **B** On the right.

   C On the right if you're right-handed. **D** On the left if you're right-handed.

6 Why might right-handers find typing more tiring than left-handers?

   A The number key pad is on the wrong side. **B** The mouse is on the right-hand side.

   C Keyboards are badly designed. **D** More keys are pressed with the left hand.

7 What happens when Melanie Croft uses normal scissors to cut things?

   A It hurts. **B** It is annoying. **C** She drops them. **D** They don't work.

8 What is meant by *smudge* in line 86?

   A break **B** produce too much ink **C** stop working **D** make a mess with wet ink

---

The word "sinister" used to mean left-handed. In Roman times left-handedness was believed to be unlucky and, remarkably, connections with devilishness persisted until fairly recently.

Thankfully, the 10% of the population who were once considered to hold pencils, cutlery and other implements "the wrong way round" are no longer likely to get their knuckles rapped in schools or have their left hands tied behind their backs by way of punishment. But modern living is still frustratingly geared to the right-handed majority.

Professor Stanley Cohen, a Canadian psychologist, claims that left-handers are 89% more accident prone than right-handed people and 25% more likely to have an accident in the workplace. This is hardly surprising in a world where left-handed office-workers have to make do with office equipment that not only make their lives difficult, but sometimes dangerous, too.

Nikki Behar is secretary to two heads of department at Manchester College of Arts and Technology. She is a typical example of an inventive and determined left-hander. "Over the years, I have had to adapt to what is there," she says. "I have been doing it for so long, I have reworked the ergonomics of the office so that they fit in with my left-handedness."

Most office desks have drawers on the right, but Nikki made sure hers were on the left. "In my previous office, they were on my right and I had to open them with my right hand or turn my chair, or cross my left hand over my stomach. Now I can open them in two seconds flat."

If telephones are positioned on the "wrong" side, it can be difficult to talk and write at the same time. Heather Bebbington, secretary to one of the senior vice-presidents at Zeneca Pharmaceuticals in Cheshire, has had phone cables lengthened to reach equipment on her left. She has also adjusted her computer equipment. "I now have my computer mouse set up for left-hand use because it was giving me wrist problems before. But it is slightly irritating if I work at someone else's desk and have to change it round."

Although 57% of typing is done with the left hand, when left-handers use the numerics pad on the keyboard, they must cross the left hand over to the right in an awkward manoeuvre. But keyboards that have numerics pads on the left make life a lot easier. Bruce Whiting, managing director of The Keyboard Company in Stroud, says his company sells around 1,000 left-handed keyboards each year. Few companies, however, are aware of their existence. "People tend to use the keyboards and the mice they are given," he says.

Right-handers tend not to think about the design of little objects such as pencil sharpeners, which can cause not only frustration but physical pain for others: left-handed pencil sharpeners turn anti-clockwise and scissors have reverse-engineered blades. "I find it almost impossible to cut with right-handed scissors because of the pain," says Melanie Croft. Left-handed workers using right-handed scissors have to force the blades apart to cut and the top blade obscures their cutting line.

When Heather Bebbington uses a ring binder, the rings are obstructed and press into her hands, so she turns the binder upside-down to put papers in. Left-handed secretaries also tend to file documents with headings on the right rather than left, which can confuse colleagues.

Another daily problem is writing with ink pens and ballpens, which are liable to smudge. "You drag your hands across what you have written and end up by getting them filthy. I use rolling writers because they have a larger ball and quick-drying ink," says Bebbington.

So be sympathetic to your left-handed peers and request special stocks for the stationery cupboard. "Left-handers are very easy to spot," says Melanie Croft, "as all their bits and pieces are on the left."

19.3 Adverbs and word order GRAMMAR REVIEW

Complete the second sentence so that it has a similar meaning to the first sentence, using the word in bold. Use between two and five words, including the word given. Don't change the word given.

1 It's very unusual for her to speak to me.

ever She .... to me.

2 It's going to be his first visit to the USA.

never He .... to America before.

3 I'll only have a bit more work to do after lunch.

nearly By lunchtime I .... my work.

4 I expect to go on holiday in August.

probably I .... a holiday in August.

5 I promise to let you know where I'm living.

certainly I .... you my address.

6 Warm weather like this is unusual in February.

usually It is .... this in February.

7 We were surprised when the door slammed shut.

suddenly The door ....

8 Don't put an adverb between a verb and direct object.

normally An adverb .... go between a verb and a direct object.

19.4 Verbs and idioms REVISION

This exercise revises some of the Verbs and idioms in 15.7, 16.7, 17.6, 18.6 and 19.7. in the Student's Book.

Complete the second sentence so that it has a similar meaning to the first sentence, using the word in bold. Use between two and five words, including the word given. Don't change the word given.

1 She used to like me, but not any more apparently.

gone She seems to .... me.

2 That's an unusual word, I don't think I have seen it before.

come I .... that word before.

3 Could you please explain that again?

going Would you mind .... that again?

4 They discouraged me from entering the race.

put They .... going in for the race.

5 The race was cancelled because of the bad weather.

called The organisers .... because the weather was bad.

6 I have no more paper.

run I .... paper.

7 He was raised by his aunt and uncle.

brought His aunt and uncle ....

8 I eat too much chocolate – I should eat less.

cut I should .... the amount of chocolate I eat.

9 We had to cancel our holiday at the last minute.

fell Our holiday plans .... at the last minute.

10 I apologise for arriving late and disappointing you.

let I'm sorry that .... by not turning up on time.

11 You borrowed a book from me, when do you think you'll return it?

bring I lent you a book last month, when are you .... ?

12 They had a row last year and they are no longer on speaking terms.

fell They haven't spoken since .... each other last year.

19.5 Paper 3: Use of English   EXAM TECHNIQUES

 A   Read this information and advice on the Use of English paper.

There are 5 Parts to the Use of English paper, which lasts 75 minutes. Don't spend longer than 15 minutes on any single part.
Part 1 (Questions 1–15) is a text with 15 gaps to fill. You have to choose the most suitable word from a choice of 4 possibles.
Part 2 (Questions 16–30) is a text with 15 gaps to fill. You have to choose the best word to fit each gap.
Part 3 (Questions 31–40) is a series of sentences which you have to rewrite using the word given. Each sentence is worth two marks, so you can get one mark for a partly correct answer.
Part 4 (Questions 41–55) – see **B** below.
Part 5 (Questions 56–65) is a text with missing words. You have to change the word given to fill each gap by forming a suitable word.

Correct spelling is essential.
If you don't know an answer: guess. Don't leave any blanks on the Answer sheet.
If you have time to spare at the end, double-check your answers.
In the exam there are sure to be a few questions you can't answer. Don't worry about this – you don't need to get 100% to get a good grade. If you really don't know, then guess. Even a silly guess is better than a blank.

> There are likely to be about 3–5 correct lines out of 15. Look again at the ones you think are correct if you have more than that.

B   Do this Error correction exercise in less than 15 minutes. Time yourself.

For Questions 41–55, read the text below and look carefully at each line. Some of the lines are correct, and some have a word which shouldn't be there.
If a line is correct put a tick (✓) by the number (in the exam, on a separate Answer sheet). If a line has a word which should not be there, write the word (on a separate Answer sheet in the exam). There are two examples at the beginning (0 and 00).

> The missing words may be articles, prepositions, adverbs or auxiliary verbs – or other words.

Shyness

0	According to experts, shyness is a growing problem in the modern world. This is	✓
00	said to be due to our loss of these social skills, which in turn is due to our increasing	these
41	dependence on computers and telephones for communicating with other	
42	people. To make up matters worse we only exchange information and our emotions are	
43	suppressed. Consequently there is less face-to-face and contact between people nowadays.	
44	Over a half the people in the world consider themselves to be shy, according to a	
45	leading expert. Shy people don't just find it hard to deal with other people but	
46	they often feel that they are inadequate and blame on themselves whenever	
47	anything goes on wrong, rather than looking for other causes.	
48	Another cause of shyness may be the way the children are treated when they are	
49	growing up. Children who are made to feel that the world is not a dangerous place	
50	and that probably other people are likely to take advantage of them or cheat them	
51	may well become shy adults. Children who are made to feel they are special and	
52	that other people are like them are more likely to be confident adults.	
53	Other experts say that the electronic age is rarely good for shy people. It gives them a	
54	chance to communicate with others without the potential embarrassment of	
55	face-to-face contact when they have to speak to strangers people.	

Paper 2: Writing – Part 2
EXAM TECHNIQUES

A Here is some information about how the Writing paper is marked.

> Each answer in the Writing paper is read by an examiner and awarded a mark according to this scheme:
>
> **5 'Full realisation of task'**
> All content points included. Wide range of grammar and vocabulary. Hardly any errors. Well-organised ideas. Style appropriate for the reader. Achieves a very positive effect on the reader.
>
> **4 'Good realisation of task'**
> All major content points included, apart from a few minor ones. Good range of grammar and vocabulary. Not many errors. Clearly-organised ideas. Style mostly appropriate for the reader. Achieves a positive effect on the reader.
>
> **3 'Reasonable realisation of task'**
> All major content points included, apart from a few minor ones. Adequate range of grammar and vocabulary. Some errors, but they don't impede communication. Adequately organised ideas. Style reasonably appropriate for the reader. Achieves a satisfactory effect on the reader.
>
> **2 'Inadequate realisation of task'**
> Some major content points omitted and/or some irrelevant material. Limited range of grammar and vocabulary. Some distracting errors and some that obscure communication. Inadequately organised ideas. Style not really appropriate for the reader. Message not clearly communicated to the reader.
>
> **1 'Poor attempt at task'**
> Many major content points omitted and/or considerable irrelevant material. Narrow range of grammar and vocabulary. Frequent errors which obscure communication. Lack of organisation. No awareness of appropriate style. Very negative effect on the reader.
>
> **0 'Too little language for assessment'**
> Fewer than 50 words and/or illegible.

B
1 Choose one question.
2 Make notes.
3 Write your answer, leaving wide margins and 2–3 lines between each paragraph.
4 Check your work and correct the mistakes you made.

> Write an answer to one of the Questions **2–4** in this part. Write your answer in 120–180 words in an appropriate style.
>
> **2** A close friend of yours invited you to a big party last week. Two families were celebrating six birthdays: two 18th birthdays, two 21st birthdays and two 50th birthdays. 500 guests watched a circus show in a big tent, where there was dancing to a live band afterwards. Another friend, who lives abroad, was unable to come to the party. Describe the party **and** include some details of the people who were there. Do not write any addresses.
> Write your **letter**.
>
> **3** People in wheelchairs find it difficult to use some of the facilities in your school or college. The Principal has asked you to write a report on this. Describe these difficulties **and** recommend changes that could be made to the buildings and equipment so that people in wheelchairs have better access.
> Write your **report**.
>
> **4** Your teacher has asked you to write a composition on this topic, with reference to your own experiences of computers, e-mail and the Internet.
> *The electronic age is having a harmful effect on people*
> Write your **composition**.

Good luck in the exam!
Try to do your best, and show the examiners what you know. Do a complete Practice test before the exam – and time how long it takes you to do each paper.

Compare your work with the model versions on page 107.

Model compositions

1.7 Mobile phones

Which points in this composition did you make in yours? Which points did you not make?

> I love mobile phones because they are really cool. They are small and light enough to carry around in your pocket or bag so you can always keep in touch with your friends. Some of them are very pretty as well and have a selection of amusing or witty ringing tones which you can choose to suit your mood or location.
>
> It's great to be able to call no matter where you are e.g. travelling on the train or the bus, when you're shopping or even up a mountain. They are vital for emergencies when there is no land phone available and parents think they're useful for keeping track of their teenagers on a night out.
>
> Although I'm not in business, I imagine they are absolutely essential for business people travelling. They can keep in frequent contact with their office, pick up their messages and carry on as if they were at their desk.
>
> Mobile phones are sometimes misused but our lives have now developed around them and life without them would be dull.
>
> *174 words*

> I hate mobile phones because of the way people use them. People seem to believe they have to shout if they are on their mobile and that the rest of the world is really interested in their very dull business. They forget they are in a public place and that others may be offended by the volume and content of their call. People use them for what are obviously insignificant calls not emergencies.
>
> It's not just <u>how</u> they are used but <u>where</u> they are used. If you go on a train, you can be sure that your efforts in concentrating on a book or listening to music will be interrupted the entire journey by mobile phone calls being made and received. Cars are another favourite and dangerous place where you see people on their phones. How can a driver give proper attention to the road if s/he is deep in conversation? How can s/he operate the steering and gears safely if one hand (and most of the brain) is engaged elsewhere?
>
> I would ban mobiles from all public places.   *179 words*

2.7 Please send me a refund . . .

One important point is missing from this letter. What is it?

> Dear Sir/Madame
>
> Last week I received from you a pair of designer jeans order number CG32980 costing £29.99. I am returning the jeans to you, which have been worn only once, as I am dissatisfied with the product.
>
> Firstly, your advertisement describes the jeans as having rivet pockets. When I opened my package there were no rivets on any of the back pockets.
>
> Your catalogue also claims that the jeans are of high quality but in fact they are of sub-standard quality. The first time I wore them the side seam tore when I bent down to pick something up and the zip broke as soon as I pulled it.
>
> In addition, I was charged £29.99 which is £10 more expensive than the price quoted in your advertisement.
>
> Yours faithfully,   *131 words*

3.7 Telling a story

One sentence in this story needs to be improved Which one is it?

> We were looking forward to a day out in the mountains. First, we were going to catch the steamer across the lake. We got there with, we thought, ten minutes to spare, but just as we were parking the car we saw the boat was about to leave. We ran as fast as we could, but it was no use – we had missed it and there wasn't another till the afternoon.
>
> We were so disappointed – the boat was going to take us to the end of the lake where we would get on the cable car to the top of the mountain. Now this was out of the question. We wondered what to do. Should we just give up, get in the car and drive home? No, we decided to make the best of it and walk round the lake.
>
> We walked round the lake and this made us feel more cheerful until lunchtime when it started to rain and this made us feel less cheerful. We sheltered under a tree to eat our sandwiches, and then we turned back – we were absolutely soaked by the time we got back. What a day!   *191 words*

4.8 Dear Ms Green ...

One important point is missing from this letter.
What is it?

Dear Ms Green,

  Thank you for your interest in our Fun
Run.

  In answer to your questions regarding the
course and arrangements for the race, I
hope you find the following information
useful.

  The course is fairly level but there is
one steep hill up and then down and as it
is circular, runners may choose to do 2 km,
once round the circuit, or 4 km, twice
round the same circuit.

  It is very generous of you to offer your
firm's first aid team and we are delighted
to accept your offer. Thank you also for
offering to donate T-shirts to all
participants. However, I am sorry to tell
you that I have already arranged T-shirts
with another firm supporting the run. Would
you by any chance be willing instead to
sponsor refreshments during and after the
run?

  I enclose two sponsorship forms and you
may photocopy as many as you like.

  Again, thank you for writing to me. We
look forward to cooperating with you on the
arrangements mentioned above.

Yours sincerely,   *174 words*

5.7 Pets

One point in favour and one point against are in
the wrong parts of the composition. Which ones
are they?

  Pets come in all shapes and sizes. Some
require a lot more attention than others
and give proportionately more back to their
owners.

  Dogs and cats provide companionship and
something warm to cuddle if you're feeling
down: very good for your stress levels.

  Some pets can also be destructive,
causing damage to your furniture, carpets
and garden. A dog or a pony also encourages
you to take exercise as they have to be
exercised if they are to remain healthy.
This in turn is good for your health,
benefiting your heart and general fitness.

  On the other hand, pets can be expensive.
Their food can add substantially to the
household budget. There are also vets' fees
which are extremely costly. Your pet will
always love you even if the whole world
seems to be against you. Pets mean
responsibility too. You can't just go on
holiday when you feel like it. You have to
make arrangements for someone to look after
your animals and that too can be expensive.
Think carefully before getting a pet.
                                  175 words

6.7 What do you recommend?

There are two points which don't need to be in this
letter. What are they?

Dear Bob,

  Thanks for your letter and the invitation
to join you on your tour of the country.
I'd love to come along as I'm free that
weekend.

  Here are the results of my research about
self-drive and chauffeur-driven mini-buses.
There are two practical and financially
realistic options.

  First of all Excelsior is a self-drive
hire company. They offer a 12-seater
minibus. It costs £140 for two days (a
special weekend rate) with unlimited
mileage. I think there would be plenty of
room for us all in this one. They do also
offer an 8-seater bus but it's a bit
cramped and costs £99 for two days and
anyway if you booked it, I wouldn't be able
to come along!

  Pullman offers chauffeur driven buses and
limousines. I think their best option would
be the 10-seater luxury minibus for £310.
Although it's more expensive than the
standard bus, it has really comfortable
seats and big windows so you'd get a good
view of the countryside. The stretch limo
can take up to ten people and it's really
cool but probably not very practical. I
actually think paying for a chauffeur-
driven vehicle would be better than self-
drive as it would be far more relaxing and
the drivers presumably know the area well
and could take us to the most interesting
and scenic sites.

Look forward to seeing you,
Love,   *228 words*

7.7 A safe place to live?

This composition is too long for an exam answer
(232 words). Decide which sentence to delete to
bring it down to under 180 words.

  I can't agree that life is more dangerous
today. If we just look at health issues,
it's certain that more than half of the
population would not have survived various
diseases or medical conditions 200 years
ago.

  200 years ago many would have died at
birth along with their mothers. Some would
not have survived childhood. Others who
managed to escape serious illness in their
youth, would have died in their late
twenties through a hard life of never-
ending labour. People also died of shock
after being operated on without
anaesthetic, or from infection afterwards.

  Car travel is often said to be the cause
of millions of deaths worldwide yet the
roads of 18th century cities were infamous
for their dangers. If you didn't get run

over by a horse, you could be attacked by street robbers who claimed many victims. You might have had a piece of furniture or piles of rubbish thrown out of a window on top of your head. Or soldiers might have arrested you and forced you to join the army.

The home was a dark and dangerous place for most of the population. Before electricity, candles and fire were used for light, cooking and heating and fuel was in short supply. People got burnt with boiling water and died in fires. In the gloomy rooms with uneven floors, people often fell and broke bones or worse. *232 words*

the way: Siros, Naxos, Paros. It was a wonderful journey.

We spent 3 days on Santorini, visiting the Minoan ruins at Akrotiri, walking along the precipitous edge of the island (it's an old volcanic crater) and of course lying on the black sand beaches soaking up the sun. After that we visited several more islands, including Ios and Naxos. The holiday was relaxing and varied, and the weather was excellent the whole time. May I recommend that you follow the same course of action next summer.

I look forward to your earliest reply,
Love, *193 words*

8.8 Free life membership!

There are two important points missing from this letter. What are they?

You can have a healthy bank balance, a fast car, the latest fashions etc. but if you don't have good health you can't enjoy any of it. It's the most important thing in your life. So you must look after it.

Keeping fit helps to maintain a healthy lifestyle; you can work out your stress while working on your heart, stamina, flexibility and strength. We all know that exercise releases happy chemicals into our bodies, keeping depression away.
Personally, I really feel good after some energetic exercise. If you are fit you can fight off infection much better too.

Eating healthily maintains fitness, guards against disease and can also help to keep you in shape. If I were a life member of Renaissance I would spend an hour a day working out in the weights room because this is the most time-efficient way of getting fit. *146 words*

9.7 A great holiday

This is supposed to be a letter to a friend. There are three sentences in the letter that are more suitable for a formal business letter. What are they? What should Tom have written instead?

Dear Val,

With reference to your letter of 15/9 I should like to thank you for your kind enquiries about my health. I'm absolutely fine and have just had a brilliant holiday in the Greek islands.

We flew to Athens and then headed off for the port at Piraeus. From there we got a ferry going as far as Santorini in the Cycladic Islands. You've seen the photos of Greek seascapes? Well, this was better than the photos. Dark blue sea, flying fish and dolphins, dark blue sky, picturesque islands dotted with whitewashed houses.
We called in at various island ports on

10.9 A birthday celebration

In this letter to the restaurant manager, there are two irrelevant sentences which make the letter too long. Cross them out.

Dear Mr Green,

A party of 20 from the Acme language school would like to come to your restaurant on Friday March 12 for a birthday celebration. Is it all right if we arrive at about 9.45? We can't be there before then because we have to attend an extra evening lesson at school. We would be happy to finish at about midnight.

We wonder whether you would be willing to let us make some changes to your advertised menu if we order the courses in advance and limit our choice. Could we order three courses per person at £9 per head instead of £11.99 as in your menu? The reason for this is that some of our group have a very limited budget and just can't manage £12 for a meal. Would it be possible for us to have a different starter? If you are agreeable to this proposal, the order would be:

    20 Greek salads
    15 Chicken Madras with rice
    5 Nut and mushroom roast with brown rice
    20 Apple and Blackberry pie

Do you have a private room or separate dining area where we can play music and sing? Finally, is access to the restaurant easy as one of the guests will be in a wheelchair?

Please let me know your response to my requests. *218 words*

11.6 Co-educational or single-sex schools?

This composition is difficult to read because it isn't separated into paragraphs. Decide where to break it up into shorter paragraphs, to make it easier to read.

Many schoolboys are noisy and badly-behaved. They disturb the class and destroy the concentration of the other pupils. The reason for this type of behaviour is because they are trying to impress each other with their disregard for authority or, when they are older, because they want to show off to the girls. Having boys in the class can adversely affect girls' learning. They don't ask questions and don't get the teacher's attention. In a single-sex environment, girls compete with each other and want to be top but mixed with boys they don't want to appear competitive or clever. On the other hand, boys and girls educated together socialise on a daily basis and thus have more realistic expectations of each other. Generally, it is better for boys to be educated with girls but not so good for girls. *139 words*

12.8 I'm sorry you missed the end . . .

The second paragraph of this letter is one, very long sentence. Decide where to split it into several shorter sentences.

Dear Viv,

Just thought I'd tell you the end of the film as you had to leave. Well you remember at the beginning there was a revolution in an unnamed African country and the heroine, who was a nurse, returned home to see her husband being dragged off and beaten by the military. There were scenes of life in the country, always accompanied by a commentary of traditional music.

After you left, the scene moved to Europe but we weren't sure where because there was no dialogue for ages and it was very unclear, but it turned out to be Italy, where the heroine was studying to be a doctor and working as housekeeper for a pianist and she also had a room in his house, which was full of the sound of classical music.

The pianist fell in love with her and to please her sold all his possessions to get money to get her husband out of prison. She had rejected his love but on the day that her husband was due to arrive in Rome she realised she loved the pianist. *182 words*

13.6 Paper 2: Writing – Part 2

Compare your answer with one of these. (There are no mistakes in these answers.)

Model letter

Dear Aunt and Uncle,

I am writing to tell you about my marvellous holiday. We flew to Rome where we boarded the coach that was to take us all over Umbria and Tuscany. We stayed first at Bolsena and went for walks in the countryside, took a boat trip on the lake and visited Orvieto and Viterbo. We also ate delicious meals and drank the splendid local white wine.

We then moved on to Assisi. This is a town with a remarkably peaceful atmosphere as well as the most stunning architecture and art. We admired the frescoes in both Basilicas. Our next stop was Siena and the highlight of the trip. The preservation of the mediaeval town and its innumerable frescoes is astonishing and to be able to sit at a café in the Campo looking on a scene that has been unchanged for 600 years was quite an experience.

I appreciated the opportunity to see for myself the art that I have been studying through reproductions. Thank you so much for helping me to go on this trip. It will really help in my work. *186 words*

Model composition

I know it's hard to believe, but I actually drove a jumbo jet! I was on my way from Singapore to Sydney and was feeling rather restless as I had already been travelling for 9 hours. We refuelled in Singapore and were due to arrive in Sydney in four to five hours.

I was chatting to one of the stewards and said that I'd love to go up front with the captain and have a look at the controls and the view from the cockpit. He said he would see if it was possible. About ten minutes later he came back and indicated I should follow him. Most of the other passengers were sleeping even though day was dawning.

I went into the cockpit and met the captain and co-pilot. I just expected to stand there for a few minutes and look around when the captain offered me his seat! I was astonished but accepted. He placed my hands on the controls and said "you're in charge." It was a thrill to think I was driving this huge machine with its 400 passengers. *183 words*

Model report

To attract young people in the first place we must stock magazines and books of interest to them. I suggest a poster outside announcing the titles of music, film, video, football etc. magazines at a special introductory price for first-time customers. Once they have come into the shop they will then see the other attractions.

Also advertise discounts on local radio and press for the under-16's on all books purchased in the next month.

Operate an exchange scheme where they can trade old books for new at a special price.

We could possibly set up a school stationery section where they can buy all the pens, paper, pencils etc. they need for school on their way to school.

Install a Youth section in the shop where books and magazines interesting to them are on display. Invite them to come and sit (in the comfy chairs provided), to meet their friends and browse.
152 words

Compare your composition or letter with one of these. (There are no mistakes in these answers.)

5a Model composition

Wuthering Heights

There are advantages and disadvantages to reading a great work of literature in translation or in a simplified original version.

One of the advantages of a simplified version is that it makes it easier to follow a complicated story. This is certainly the case with Wuthering Heights. The way that the story starts is confusing even in a simplified version. It is not clear who the various Catherines are, what point in time we are at or what relationship the narrator has to Heathcliff. I was really gripped by the story and although it was simplified, it was still quite a challenge.

However, the reasons for Catherine's behaviour towards Linton didn't seem too clear in this version. I read it in translation and felt that I had a much better understanding of why Linton acted as he did. Also the landscape seemed to play an important role which it didn't have in the simplified version.
154 words

5b Model letter

Dear Hilary,

I've just read 'The Old Man and the Sea' by Ernest Hemingway and loved it. It was great to be able to read a famous book in English.

As you may know it's a very simple but powerful story of an old Cuban fisherman's attempt to catch a huge marlin by himself. There is also a young boy in the story and although he is not with the old man the relationship between the two plays an

important role. It's also the story of a heroic fight against bad luck and of man alone against the power of nature. I'm keen on fishing and sailing myself so I could understand to some extent how he felt.

The language is very straightforward and simple because it represents the thoughts and speech of a simple man. We can follow every emotion the man has and share in his hope, fear, determination and final sadness. I think you would really enjoy it.
159 words

14.7 A summer job

This letter contains two sentences with irrelevant information and two pieces of important information are missing.

Dear Sir/Madam,

I am writing to apply for the post of summer beach assistant. I finished High School nearly two years ago and am now in the second year of my Sports Studies course at Nuffield University.

I think I would be suited to the work as I enjoy meeting people, I like being outside and am not afraid of physical work. I am pretty fit as I am training to be a sports teacher. I have worked with children while on my course and also as a waiter in a holiday hotel. I can also play the piano quite well.

Please can you tell me during which period exactly you require beach assistants and also what the rates of pay are?

Yours faithfully,
120 words

15.7 What can go wrong?

This report is fine, apart from three spelling mistakes. Can you find them?

Faulty VCR

PLAY
When you attempt to <u>play</u>, the VCR works for 10 to 15 minutes but then the picture brakes up and the recording jumps. We tried adjusting the tracking but it didn't make any difference. If you stop the machine and restrat, it's OK for another 10 to 15 minutes but then the problem reappears. This fault occurs only with commercial tapes not those recorded on the VCR.

RECORD
There is also a problem with the <u>record</u> facility: the timer control doesn't work. If you set the machine to record at a certin time it always records Channel 1. It is impossible to record any other channel.

REMOTE CONTROL
You have to press the buttons very hard to get any results. The <u>pause</u> button does not work. We have fitted <u>a new</u> battery but it doesn't make any difference.
140 words

16.6 A letter to the editor

This letter is fine, apart from three mistakes using Capital letters. Can you find them?

Dear sir/Madam,

I am writing to comment on your plans to alter your newspaper's style and content.

Although I agree with the idea of being positive and reporting 'good' news, I am not quite sure that it is so easy to define good news. What is good to one person may be bad to another. And as for your proposal to carry only good news in the main story on the front page, this is ridiculous. the main story should report the most important event of the day, good or bad.

I don't want any more sports news as there is too much in the paper already. Nor do I think that your reviewers should leave their opinions out of the reviews. I like To read what someone else thinks as this helps me decide which films I see or books I read. Your editorials should continue as they are, giving all the arguments in favour or against on the issue under discussion.

I'm all in favour of a new cartoon page and Jokes of the Day.   *175 words*

17.7 Paper 2: Writing – Part 2

These model answers are fine, apart from one spelling mistake in each. Can you find them?

Model article

Travel broadens the mind or at least that's what we hope. We can experience the climate, the sounds, the smells, the food for ourselves and know what it is like to be a Pacific islander or an Inuit.

If we are lucky and have worthwhile experiences, we can find ourselves in contact with a culture and a people that we have only read about. Unfortunately, in the days of 5-star international hotels located on the best beach or on the best land in the city, travellers are more often than not kept apart from the locals. The locals are discouraged from mixing with visitors except as payed workers. So the experience of learning about another society is in effect diluted through the imported comforts of home. Just the weather and the view are different.

World travel has always had two-way influences and we would be naïve to expect anything else. Yet today, the effects of international tourism seem to be to the detriment of developing countries in spite of the multiple health jabs, cramped conditions on long-haul flights and severe jet-lag endured by the western traveller.

186 words

Model story

Have you ever been so far away from home, to a place so outlandish, unusual or simply remote that your whole world seems upside down? Well, I have.

It was two years ago when I decided to throw over my job, sell the flat, the car, the cat, leave Putney far behind me and make for the wild unknown (to me at least) expanses of northern Norway. It was the middle of summer, you understand, so I wasn't planning to test myself in the darkness of an Arctic winter.

I spent my first weeks in the village of Reine in the Lofoten Islands, 160 km inside the Arctic Circle, in a dazzled blur of unsleeping nights and dozy days, enjoying the freedom, the fresh, surprisingly warm air but feeling like a Martian.

One morning, or maybe it was late evening – difficult to tell in this land of the midnight sun – I hired a small boat to visit a nearby island.

I saw another craft approching. We waved a greeting. "Hi, Frankie!" said the occupant. Jem from Human Resources! It's an annoyingly small world.   *184 words*

Model report

Most visitors are impressed with the large number of historical buildings in the town and those a short journey away in rural locations. Their state of preservation is admired as are the many changing exhibitions which take place, particularly in the castle. The major complaint is about opening hours and accessibility for disabled visitors. I suggest opening hours be extended by at least an hour during the summer months and that buildings open on Sunday mornings. There are not enough wheelchair ramps and lifts should be installed wherever possible.

The sporting facilities in the town are particularly popular, especially the swimming pools. However, there has been criticism of the golf course, which is poorly maintained and overrun by dogs. This is a very valuable amenity and attracts many overseas visitors so we raelly must bring it up to the highest standard. I suggest we charge more per round, employ more groundsmen (staff) and restrict access to dog owners to Sunday afternoons.

161 words

18.6 An exhibition

This letter should be divided into paragraphs. Where should it be split to make four short paragraphs?

Dear Bob,

    I am writing to tell you about an exhibition at the Serpentine Gallery that you won't want to miss. It's a Bridget Riley show, her paintings from the 1960s and 70s. I know you love her work. So why don't we combine a visit to the exhibition with lunch and the chance to spend the day together? I know it's a long way to come for a day but the exhibition is free and there's a special offer on the trains. If you get a day return on any Saturday in July, the fare is only £39, which is less than half the price of the normal fare. However, you must book it in advance. I've checked on the trains and there are several that would get you into King's Cross before midday. I think the 07.30 from Newcastle arriving at 10.38 would be the best. Please write and let me know if you're interested and if so which train you will be getting. I'll meet you at King's Cross. Look forward to hearing from you.

Love,   *179 words*

19.6 Paper 2: Writing – Part 2

Each of these answers would get marks in Band 5 or 4. (There are no mistakes in these answers.)

Model letter

Dear Phil,

    I know you were invited to Emma's 18th and were unable to come so I'll tell you about it. It was really amazing because it wasn't just Emma's party but a combined party for six people.

    There were two families involved who have been friends for years: two of the daughters were celebrating their 21st, two their 18th and the two mothers their 50th. They held the party in a big tent where there was a circus from 7 until 9. The 500 guests were able to dance to a live band until about 2 am and there was a buffet and a barbecue and loads of drink.

    I saw John and Martha from school and Peter, James and Henry had just got back from their trip 'down-under' and were full of their adventures. I also caught sight of Amy dancing with a rather handsome guy but I didn't manage to speak to her.

    Emma was really sorry you couldn't come and had to miss such a brilliant party.

Love,   *170 words*

Model report

    Poor wheelchair access is causing problems for students in the science labs. Work benches are too high and students can't reach the equipment to carry out experiments. The floor behind one of the benches could be raised by about 20 cms with ramps at either end.

    There are also some problems for wheelchair users who want to use the payphone situated on the first floor. The phone is actually three steps up from the main floor on a kind of platform. This is completely inaccessible for wheelchair users. The phone should be positioned on the main floor.

    The doors to the Cafeteria are far too narrow for wheelchairs when there are a lot of people queuing and they are also difficult to open. The doorway should be widened and the doors should open automatically.   *135 words*

Model composition

    I can't agree with this statement. It is true that some people spend hours over their computers, playing games, sending and receiving e-mail and surfing the Net, but what harm does this do?

    One criticism is that people no longer go out and socialise but in fact the Internet allows you to contact more people in more countries than ever before. The difference is that you socialise on-line rather than in person. People are developing friendships through the Internet and are finding out more about how foreigners live and think directly.

    Playing computer games is a pastime like any other. People used to collect stamps or cigarette cards or build models but now they play computer games. If this was their only activity perhaps it would be worrying but people still go to work, go to school, meet their friends, exchange and discuss the games with their friends.

    E-mail has led to far more letter writing and a dying art has been brought back to life.   *166 words*

Irregular verb table

infinitive · past · past participle

be · was/were · been
bear · bore · born
beat · beat · beaten
become · became · become
begin · began · begun
bend · bent · bent
bet · bet · bet
bite · bit · bitten
blow · blew · blown
break · broke · broken
breed · bred · bred
bring · brought · brought
build · built · built
burst · burst · burst
buy · bought · bought
catch · caught · caught
choose · chose · chosen
cling · clung · clung
come · came · come
cost · cost · cost
creep · crept · crept
cut · cut · cut
deal · dealt · dealt
dig · dug · dug
draw · drew · drawn
drink · drank · drunk
drive · drove · driven
eat · ate · eaten
fall · fell · fallen
feed · fed · fed
feel · felt · felt
fight · fought · fought
find · found · found
flee · fled · fled
fling · flung · flung
fly · flew · flown
forbid · forbade · forbidden
forget · forgot · forgotten
forgive · forgave · forgiven
freeze · froze · frozen

get · got · got
give · gave · given
go · went · gone
grind · ground · ground
grow · grew · grown
have · had · had
hear · heard · heard
hide · hid · hidden
hit · hit · hit
hold · held · held
hurt · hurt · hurt
keep · kept · kept
know · knew · known
lay · laid · laid
lead · led · led
leave · left · left
lend · lent · lent
let · let · let
lie · lay · lain
lie · lied · lied
lose · lost · lost
make · made · made
mean · meant · meant
meet · met · met
pay · paid · paid
put · put · put
quit · quit · quit
read · read · read
ride · rode · ridden
ring · rang · rung
rise · rose · risen
run · ran · run
say · said · said
see · saw · seen
seek · sought · sought
sell · sold · sold
send · sent · sent
set · set · set
shake · shook · shaken
shed · shed · shed

shine · shone · shone
shoot · shot · shot
show · showed · shown
shrink · shrank · shrunk
shut · shut · shut
sing · sang · sung
sink · sank · sunk
sit · sat · sat
sleep · slept · slept
slide · slid · slid
speak · spoke · spoken
spend · spent · spent
spread · spread · spread
spring · sprang · sprung
stand · stood · stood
steal · stole · stolen
stick · stuck · stuck
sting · stung · stung
strike · struck · struck
swear · swore · sworn
sweep · swept · swept
swim · swam · swum
swing · swung · swung
take · took · taken
teach · taught · taught
tear · tore · torn
tell · told · told
think · thought · thought
throw · threw · thrown
thrust · thrust · thrust
tread · trod · trod
understand · understood · understood
wake · woke · woken
wear · worn · worn
weep · wept · wept
win · won · won
write · wrote · written

Answers and Transcripts

Communication

1.1 Talking about language

```
                    13
   1 A B S T R A C T
   2 P R O N U N C I A T I O N
   3 A D V E R B S
   4 S Y L L A B L E S
   5 A L P H A B E T I C A L L Y
   6 M A N N E R S
 7 A C C E N T S
   8 H I G H L I G H T
   9 S U F F I X
  10 C A P I T A L
     11 G E S T U R E S
  12 P R E F I X
```

1.2 Cutting noise pollution

2 A   3 G   4 C   5 F   6 B

1.3 Word-building, synonyms and opposites

impossible   possibility   powerful (or powerless)
raindrops   headache   width   proud   fantastic
fascinating   difficult   dangerous

1.4 Present tenses

A
2 don't look like   3 drink/have have/drink
4 boils   5 speak   6 am studying
7 goes wants   8 am trying

B
2 have you been looking   3 have been   4 costs
5 have been waiting   6 has drunk   7 am going
8 Do/Would you prefer

1.6 Free phone calls – with commercials

1 U   2 S + B   3 U   4 U   5 S   6 B
7 S   8 B

TRANSCRIPT   *3 minutes 30 seconds*

PRESENTER: Do you spend a lot of money on phone calls? You do? Well, a new scheme has been announced which gives you free phone calls. John Davis has been looking into it. John, is there such a thing as a free phone call?

JOHN: Yes, there does seem to be – if you don't mind advertisements.

PRESENTER: Hahaha. So how does it work?

JOHN: Well, this kind of scheme started some years ago in Sweden. The Swedish company Gratistelefon introduced it in northern Sweden. Callers there dial a free-phone number followed by the number they wish to contact. While they wait to be connected, a commercial is played. Each commercial costs the advertiser about 4 pence. Now, after the first minute of conversation the call is interrupted by a 10-second commercial and thereafter every three minutes.

PRESENTER: Ahhh. Have they tried this anywhere else?

JOHN: Yes, um…a similar scheme called FreeWay operates in Pittsburgh in the USA. Er…this scheme enabled private customers to build up a bank of free call time according to the number of commercials that they're prepared to endure.

For each commercial, lasting between 5 and 15 seconds, callers get a two-minute credit to phone anywhere in the United States. Now, local calls are free in the USA, so you build up a credit for long-distance calls. When the credits begin to run out, subscribers merely have to dial a free-phone number and listen to more advertisements.

Now, people signing up for the service have to fill out a questionnaire about their interests so that the advertisements can be 'tailored' to their tastes. The advertisements are 'interactive'. Callers can press specific buttons to order goods or services.

PRESENTER: And now it's our turn in the UK?

JOHN: Yes, it's called BT FreeTime. First you have to register, fill in a questionnaire and then you receive a free-phone number and PIN number to use before making BT FreeTime calls. You'll hear a 10-second advert at the beginning of the call, before you're connected, then every two minutes your call will be interrupted with another 10-second commercial. Now, the free scheme can be accessed from any fixed line phone and used to call any local or national long distance number. Calls to mobile telephones, and to premium lines and abroad…er…won't be permitted.

When customers join BT FreeTime they complete a questionnaire so the messages they hear are relevant to their interests and buying habits. The phone company will know everything about you – where you live and what you like to buy and do, so the adverts will be tailored exactly to your interests.

PRESENTER: So, it this the future for all of us? Phone calls with adverts?

JOHN: I don't think so…already mobile phone companies are offering free calls at weekends and as the costs of phoning comes down, fewer and fewer people will be prepared to have their conversations interrupted by irritating adverts.

PRESENTER: John, thank you.

At your service!

2.1 Shops and stores

Across: cheque   goods   pen   queue
credit card   map   butcher   VAT   tea
bargain   sweater

Down: fashion   assistant   newsagent
department   lift   till   counter   guarantee
cash   hat   tie   market   shop   pharmacy

2.2 Questions and question tags

A
2   if you are going shopping on Saturday?
3   when the supermarket opens?
4   where the toilets are?
5   where you bought those blue shoes?
6   how much a pair of shoes like that costs.
7   who you went to town with.
8   much money you have spent?

B
2 aren't they?   3 don't they?   4 can't we?
5 can you?   6 shall we?   7 did there?
8 didn't you?

2.3 Levis jeans

2 D   3 E   4 A   5 G   6 F   7 C

2.4 Abbreviations and numbers

A 2 February   3 Wednesday   4 information
5 approximately   6 United Kingdom   7 Square
8 Forty West Twentieth Street (in New York)

B 2 forty-four point four   3 one thousand, two hundred
and thirty-four   4 eight point five/eight and a half
5 seven and three-quarters   6 fourteen
7 seven hundred and seventy-eight   8 three million

2.5 Can I help you?

1 C   2 B   3 C   4 C   5 B

TRANSCRIPT *3 minutes*

FIRST WOMAN: Oh that's nice. Is it new?
SECOND WOMAN: Yes, do you like it?
FIRST WOMAN: Yes, it really suits you. It's just your colour.
SECOND WOMAN: I was worried that it was a bit short.
FIRST WOMAN: No, not at all. It's lovely.
SECOND WOMAN: What about the sleeves? They're a bit short, aren't they?
FIRST WOMAN: No, no, they're fine. As I said, it's lovely.
SECOND WOMAN: Oh good.

MAN: Hello, I want to change 165 US dollars into Euros.
WOMAN: Hello sir, certainly …174… I make it 175 dollars.
MAN: Oh, OK. 175 dollars then.
WOMAN: So that's 172 Euros 50 cents – less commission, which comes to 167.50.
MAN: Er…just a minute, how much is commission?
WOMAN: 2 per cent.
MAN: But 2 per cent of 172.50 isn't 5.
WOMAN: No, but there's a minimum commission charge of 5 Euros.
MAN: That's outrageous!
WOMAN: Sorry about that. Do you still want to change the money?
MAN: Yes, go ahead.

WOMAN: Can I help you?
MAN: Yes, I…er…need something for a sore throat.
WOMAN: Oh, how long have you had it?
MAN: Since the weekend.
WOMAN: Well, we have these lozenges. You suck one every hour. Or you could try this new preparation: it's an inaler. You use it every two hours. Or we have this syrup which is very good. You take a spoonful three times a day.
MAN: Which do you recommend?
WOMAN: Oh, they're all very good.
MAN: OK, er…I'll try the new one.

MAN: Next please.
WOMAN: How much will it cost to send this air mail to Canada?
MAN: Just pop it on the scales and I'll tell you. …Oh dear, it's £17.50, I'm afraid.
WOMAN: Oh, no.
MAN: Well, if you want to send it surface mail it's £8.40 – but it'll take several weeks to get there.
WOMAN: But it's only a book for my nephew – it's for his birthday next week.
MAN: A book? Oh, there's a cheaper rate for airmail Printed Papers. That's £9.55.
WOMAN: Oh good, I'll do that.
MAN: You just need to write "Printed Papers" on the top and fill in this green label with the words "Book" and put a cross in the box where it says "Gift".

MARKET TRADER: Yes, madam?
CUSTOMER: How much are these gloves?
MARKET TRADER: Those are genuine designer gloves, made in Italy. They're just £5.50 a pair.
CUSTOMER: Have you got any cheaper?
MARKET TRADER: Oh, try them on, they're lovely and warm.

CUSTOMER: Oh, they're nice. But I don't want to pay that much.
MARKET TRADER: Tell you what, here's a lovely matching scarf that I normally sell for the same price as the gloves. Now, you can have one of these scarves and the gloves for £8.
CUSTOMER: Oh, all right. Here's £10.
MARKET TRADER: Thank you. Here's £2 change. Would you like them in a bag?

2.7 Please send me a refund …

The missing point is:

```
Please send me a full refund of £29.99
plus postage.
```

3 Friends and relations

3.1 Love, marriage and families

```
                  19
        1 B I R T H D A Y
      2 M A R R I E D
      3 N I E C E
          4 D A U G H T E R
      5 G R E A T    A U N T

      6 F I A N C E
    7 F I A N C E E
    8 W E D D I N G

          9 B E S T
        10 R E L A T I V E S
   11 A N N I V E R S A R Y
        12 D I V O R C E D
      13 N E P H E W
      14 G R A N D S O N
      15 R E C E P T I O N
  16 B R O T H E R   I N   L A W
      17 L O V E
    18 M U M
```

3.2 Here comes the bride!

1 C   2 C   3 B   4 C   5 B
6 A (Carla's father, mother and sister + Greg's father, step-mother and three brothers)   7 C   8 B

3.3 Using prefixes – 1

A rearrange   pre-exam   post-lunch   overcrowded
underprepared

B 1 remarried   2 overdone/underdone
3 overestimated   4 renamed   5 pre-heated
6 reconsider   7 reappeared   8 overpriced

3.4 The past – 1

A
	forgot forgotten
wrote written	took taken
stuck stuck	heard heard
drove driven	tried tried
ran run	broke broken

B 2 met   3 described   4 entered   5 saw
6 spoke   7 proposed   8 separated   9 said
10 explained   11 spent   12 failed

3.6 A sad romance

1 T   2 T   3 F   4 T   5 F   6 T   7 T

TRANSCRIPT *2 minutes 45 seconds*

REPORTER: There was a funeral in the Greek city of Patras yesterday which brought an infinitely sad ending to a romance which has lasted for 58 years.

The story recalls the plot of the best-selling novel by Louis de Bernières, *Captain Corelli's Mandolin*. Now, in 1941, during the Second World War, Luigi Surace met and he fell in love with Angeliki Stratigou while he was serving with the Italian forces in Greece. They decided to get married when the war was over. Now, he was posted elsewhere, but he continued to write to his fiancée.

Angeliki had lost both her parents and lived with her aunt. But, sadly, her aunt disapproved of the relationship so, whenever a letter arrived from Luigi, the aunt intercepted it and she destroyed it. After several years without a reply, Luigi gave up writing.

After some years he found a wife…er… he had a son, and settled down to married life in Reggio Calabria in Southern Italy.

But Angeliki, the Greek girl he met in the war remained the love of his life. Three years ago, after the death of his wife, he set about trying to find Angeliki Stratigou.

He wrote to the town hall of Patras. The council officers there asked for the help of Nancy Pavlopoulou, a local journalist, and she found the woman he'd left behind more than a half a century earlier. She had never married. Luigi and Angeliki met, and they decided to marry. Nancy, the local journalist, was to be Ms Stratigou's maid of honour.

Luigi was due in Patras on December 22nd. He planned to spend Christmas with his fiancée and help her prepare at last for their wedding. But then, just before he was due to leave Italy, Luigi fell ill, was taken to hospital and had to postpone his trip.

Now, while he was still ill in hospital, in Italy, Angeliki was herself taken ill, and taken to hospital in Patras. Sadly she died on Saturday of a stroke at the age of 81.

The next day Nancy got home to find a telegram waiting. It had been sent by Luigi on the day his fiancée died. It said: "I am better. I am coming. Wait for me."

3.7 Telling and writing a story

Sentence to be improved:

```
We walked round the lake and this made us
feel more cheerful until lunchtime when it
started to rain and this made us feel less
cheerful.
→ By lunchtime we were feeling much more
cheerful, but then it started to rain.
```

4 Time off

4.1 Sports and leisure activities

Across: cards   music   windsurfing (+ surfing) photography   cookery   yoga   painting   darts

Down: swimming   diving   dancing   golf badminton   basketball   running   aerobics football   reading   chess   tennis   cycling waterskiing (+ skiing)

4.3 Cheese Races, 1998

2 G   3 D   4 B   5 F   6 C
7 H (A doesn't fit anywhere)

4.4 The past – 2

2 won   3 attracted   4 beat
5 has (regularly) taken part   6 had won
7 was won   8 came   9 have been held
10 were cancelled   11 were injured
12 called   13 installed   14 were (slightly) hurt
15 were (not) taken

4.5 Using prefixes – 2

2 mid-thirties   3 half-eaten   4 mid-sentence
5 self-motivated   6 half-open   7 mid-week
8 half-empty   half-full

4.6 Swimming with sharks

1 72 days   2 6 to 8   3 on the support yacht
4 5kmh   5 300 km   6 American
7 cancer research   8 emotional block   9 800 km
10 7   11 10 metres   12 "never again"

TRANSCRIPT *4 minutes 15 seconds*

ANNOUNCER: …and now over to James Morgan who is in France where Ben Lecomte has just landed after swimming across the North Atlantic. James, are you there?

JAMES: Yes, Sue. Er…I'm here in the harbour of Port Maria in Quiberon in Brittany. And we've got a huge crowd here to welcome Ben Lecomte to France, the land of his birth. Also here: his fiancée, his mother and his brothers.

Now, when Ben set out from Hyannis in Massachusetts he announced that he was going to swim right across the Atlantic in 80 days – but he's managed the swim in just 72 days. Before he set off he asked his girlfriend Trinh Dang to marry him – she said 'Yes', and Ben entered the water.

All the way across he swam on the port side of his support vessel, a 12-metre yacht, for six to eight hours each day. He ate, rested and slept aboard the yacht, getting up at 6 am, burning 9,000 calories a day and swimming in two-hour stretches.

Now, he swam an average of 5 kilometres an hour and, in the latest leg from the Azores, he's covered between 40 and 55 kilometres a day. In the beginning, he was swimming with the currents of the Gulf Stream and covering up 300 kilometres in a day… Oh, here comes Ben now. Er…Ben! Ben, congratulations! How do you feel?

BEN: …

JAMES: …Ah, well, I'm afraid I can't get to talk to Ben just now. But that gives me time to tell you a bit more about him:

Ben Lecomte is 31 years old, born in France but's now a naturalised American citizen. He lives in Austin, Texas, a long way from the ocean. When Ben's father died of cancer he decided to undertake this swim to raise money for cancer research. He trained for 6 years and swam thousands of miles, raising £100,000 before he set off on July 16th. Now, of that total, he needs about half to pay the expenses of the trip. During the swim more money's been pouring in to the website that's been following his progress day by day…

Oh, er…he's now been driven off, with his fiancée and members of his family. Ah…but here is Colleen Turner, who's Ben's spokesperson, and who was with him on the last leg of the journey. So Colleen, I expect you're relieved?

COLLEEN: Oh, you bet! But we all knew he could do it.

JAMES: Ah, but I do know that he nearly gave up back in August?

COLLEEN: The swim went well until August 20th when he started to feel a…an 'emotional block'. He had to get out of the water, so he swam 800 kilometres off his route to the Azores, about 1,500 kilometres west of Portugal. He stayed seven days to get his head together. Then he got back in the water.

For the last few weeks, the water has been extremely cold and he's had to wear gloves, which he doesn't like because he can't feel his hands going through the water. It's pretty amazing really. He's been through a lot.

JAMES: And…er…what about sharks?

COLLEEN: Well, the yacht was fitted with two loudspeakers at the bow and stern, which sent out an electro-magnetic signal which acts as a 'force field' to repel the sharks.

At one point, he was followed by a great white shark. He didn't know exactly how big it was but he could see it was moving back and forth about 10 metres below him. All he could see were its head and tail. Lecomte said 'It's a lot bigger than I am' and that was 10 metres away.

JAMES: Now Colleen, this performance has been disputed by some people who say that he spent most of his day not swimming but resting and sleeping on the support yacht, where a crew of two helped him prepare six high calorie meals a day.

COLLEEN: He gained no advantage in distance by resting on the yacht. The swim itself was a real ordeal – he had to wear two wetsuits to keep out the cold.

JAMES: And…er…is Ben going to try another swim like this?

COLLEEN: Haha…no, his first words when he waded ashore were 'Never again!'

JAMES: Colleen, thank you. And…er…do give our best wishes to Ben and his fiancée.

COLLEEN: I sure will.

4.8 Dear Ms Green …

The missing point:

```
I'm afraid that there will be no prizes as
it is a fun run and not a race.
```

5 The world around us

5.1 Nature and the weather

```
        16
1 S H O W E R
2 F O R E S T
    3 G A L E
4 P L A N T
5 L I G H T N I N G
6 D E S E R T
7 T E M P E R A T U R E
      8 F O G G Y
    9 D O L P H I N S
  10 F R O S T
11 B R E E Z E
      12 C L O U D Y
13 M A M M A L
  14 I N S E C T
15 H E A T W A V E
```

5.2 The ice-storm

2 G   3 D   4 A   5 C   6 H
7 F   (E doesn't fit anywhere)

5.3 Using prefixes – 3

(A)

	impossible	impatient
illegible	irrelevant	inappropriate
inefficient	unfortunate	
unclear	immature	
informal	inaccurate	

(B) 2 misheard   3 Unfortunately
4 inaccuracy/inaccuracies   5 inconvenience
6 unwilling   7 unable   8 disobeying

5.4 Articles and quantifiers – 1

(A) a glass/bottle/jug of water   a carton/bottle/
glass of milk   a cup/pot/can of coffee
a can/a bottle   glass/litre of beer   a bar/piece of
chocolate   a piece of information   a bottle/
glass of wine   a piece/an item of news
(*There are other possibilities too*)

(B) 2 rained so heavily/much
3 was so much traffic that / such heavy traffic that
4 many people attended
5 have as much luggage as
6 you have any accommodation
7 go to school / attend school
8 the weather will be wet/rainy

5.6 One-minute talks

1 A   2 B   3 B   4 A   5 B   6 A

TRANSCRIPT   *3 minutes*

ANGELA: You know, I don't understand why people have big fierce dogs. You know, like Dobermans or pit bull terriers. Look…look at this person here! Is he afraid of being attacked? Or does he just want other people to be frightened of him? I think it's very strange, you know, I mean the relationship people have with dogs. A dog can be a companion for someone who lives alone, or a guard dog to protect their property from criminals. But I really don't think it's fair to keep big dogs like those in a city apartment. Dogs need plenty of exercise and, well, they can't get exercise in a park because they need to run free. Look at…look at that there, I mean, a dog like that has to be on a lead all the time in a park or in the street, otherwise it'll attack people. In fact, I think too many people keep dogs in apartments – and they leave them all alone all day while they're out at work. My neighbours, for instance, they've got a big Labrador and he's out in the garden all day on his own. It's…it's just not fair on the animals. On the other hand, well, I think it's good for children to have a pet in the family. Puppies, you know, they're adorable little creatures and children love to play with them.

BILL: The trouble with puppies is that, well, they grow into dogs. And dogs, they have to be looked after, taken for walks and so on. And, well, if you have a dog you can't go away on holiday or for the weekend, unless you can get someone to look after it. And me, I just feel cheeky asking someone else to look after my pet. I…I mean, you can take your dog in a car but not usually on a train or plane or something like that. And, well, hotels often don't welcome dogs. So, well, having a dog is a bit of a responsibility. You know, you've got to think about it carefully. Now, cats: well, they're different. They don't need so much looking after, they're independent. And you can get a neighbour to feed them if you're going away. And you don't have to take them for walks, you know, they'll do that themselves. And you don't have to worry about them barking or frightening the children. You know, they're affectionate, they like to be stroked and petted – it feels nice. Well, on the other hand, if you're afraid of burglars, well, a cat isn't a very effective deterrent!

5.7 Talking for a minute: Pets

Points in the wrong parts of the composition:

```
Some pets can also be destructive, causing
damage to your furniture, carpets and
garden.
```

```
Your pet will always love you even if the
whole world seems to be against you.
```

6 Going places

6.1 Travel and transport

Across: motorway   pavement   fare   pedestrian   car   trip   brake   metro   accident   speeding   fuel   outing   journey   bypass   taxi   junction

Down: bus   roundabout   path   park   driving test   seat belt   transport   flight   cyclist

6.2 Articles – 2

1 the   2 the   3 the   4 the   5 a   6 the
7 the   8 a   9 a/the   10 a   11 a   12 a
13 the   14 the   15 a   16 a   17 the   18 a
19 a   20 the   21 the   22 the   23 a/the
24 the   25 the   26 a/the   27 the   28 a
29 the   30 the

6.4 Young drivers in California

1 D   2 C   3 F   4 E   5 B
(A doesn't fit anywhere)

6.5 People on the move

1 A   2 B   3 B   4 B   5 A

T R A N S C R I P T   *3 minutes 30 seconds*

MAN: What time are we supposed to get there?
WOMAN: I'm not sure. It's certainly taking longer than I expected.
MAN: Oh, goodness, we've stopped again. I wonder what the matter is this time.
WOMAN: Don't worry it's only another four stops.
MAN: Oh right. But next time we'll take the train. It'll be quicker.
WOMAN: But it'll cost more.

MAN: Er…excuse me.
WOMAN: Yes, can I help you.
MAN: I'm trying to find the bus station.
WOMAN: Oh it's quite near. Which way have you just come?
MAN: Well, I asked someone outside the supermarket and they told me to go to the left and then at the next junction turn left again.
WOMAN: Oh I see, that's why you're here. This is the railway station. From here you should cross over the road, here, and take the first turning on the left. Then just go on walking till the next traffic lights. It's opposite the main post office.
MAN: So it's straight on and then first left?
WOMAN: No, the other way round. First on the left, then straight on.

WOMAN: I'd like a return to Newcastle, please.
MAN: Newcastle-upon-Tyne?
WOMAN: Yes.
MAN: When're you travelling?
WOMAN: Tomorrow, and coming back on Friday.
MAN: Er…the standard return is £50, but if you're sure you'll be coming back on Friday it'll be cheaper.
WOMAN: Yes, I'm sure.
MAN: What time are you coming back?
WOMAN: There's a train from there at 8.30.
MAN: Ah, if you take that train it's £30.50 return. But if you get a later train after 10 am you can get a cheap saver return for £15.
WOMAN: Oh, well, that's sound like a good idea. The trouble is I have to back here by lunchtime, so that's no good. I have to catch the 8.30.
MAN: Fine. So that's a…

GUEST: Hello, I want to catch a bus into the centre. Is that easy to do?
RECEPTIONIST: Sure, there's a bus every ten minutes from the other side of the road.
GUEST: OK, good, thanks.
RECEPTIONIST: Sir? You need to get a ticket before you get on the bus.
GUEST: Oh, I thought I could I get one on board.
RECEPTIONIST: No, I'm afraid not. Some bus stops have a machine where you can buy a ticket, but only the ones in the city centre.
RECEPTIONIST: So what do I do?
WOMAN: You can buy a ticket from the newspaper kiosk over there. And when you get on the bus you have to put it into the machine and get it stamped. Get two if you're coming back on the bus.

TRAVEL AGENT: Can I help you?
CUSTOMER: Yes, I want to get to London. Is it cheaper by coach or by train?
TRAVEL AGENT: That all depends when you want to go there.
CUSTOMER: OK, well, I want to be there by 6 pm on Wednesday and be back here by the same time on Tuesday.
TRAVEL AGENT: All right. Um…the coach will cost £49.50 for midweek travel and the train is £59.40.
CUSTOMER: And how long does the coach take?
TRAVEL AGENT: Twice as long as the train. But I think I've got a better solution.
WOMAN: Yes?
MAN: Yes, EasyAirlines have a special fare this month. You can get flights to London and back for £55.
WOMAN: Oh right. Can I book that with you now?

6.7 What do you recommend?

Two points which don't need to be in this letter:

They do also offer an eight-seater bus but it's a bit cramped and costs £99 for two days and anyway if you booked it, I wouldn't be able to come along!

The stretch limo can take up to ten people and it's really cool but probably not very practical.

7 There's no place like home

7.1 At home

1	A	P	A	R	T	M	E	N	T
2	W	A	L	L	P	A	P	E	R
3	K	I	T	C	H	E	N		
4	M	O	V	E					
5	L	A	N	D	L	A	D	Y	
6	B	A	L	C	O	N	Y		
7	C	U	P	B	O	A	R	D	
8	S	U	B	U	R	B	S		
9	C	U	R	T	A	I	N	S	
10	D	R	A	W	E	R	S		
11	C	E	L	L	A	R			
12	S	H	E	L	F				
13	L	A	W	N					
14	C	O	T	T	A	G	E		
15	S	H	E	D					
16	W	A	R	D	R	O	B	E	
17	B	A	S	E	M	E	N	T	
18	R	E	N	T					

(19 down at top of puzzle)

7.2 Paris bus drivers in London

1 A   2 C   3 C   4 B   5 A   6 B

7.3 Spelling and pronunciation – 1: Vowels

2 route   3 passed   4 check sure   5 leant to
6 knew which   7 weak flu   8 worn

7.4 Modal verbs – 1

(A)
2 may/might   3 can't   4 Might/Could
5 have to/must   6 don't have to
7 mustn't/shouldn't   8 should

(B)
2 don't have to   3 shouldn't walk home alone
4 may/might be late   5 can't be / cannot be
6 don't need to / needn't   7 we allowed to write
8 can only be used

7.6 Welcome to Heritage Park!

1 police force   2 electric fence   3 play in the street
4 walk to school   5 worry   6 10 minutes' drive
7 24 years   8 1,000   9 142   10 2,000

T R A N S C R I P T *3 minutes 30 seconds*

REPORTER: When George Hazeldon went to France he visited Mont Saint Michel, the ancient monastery and fortress. It inspired him to create a new town in South Africa which provides the same security and sense of community. He's called it Heritage Park.

GEORGE: It's never been done in South Africa before. Er…we're building a whole town here, not just a few houses with a security guard. There will be churches and schools and shops and lakes, and its own police force of about 40 men. There's even going to be a graveyard.

REPORTER: Residents will need a pass to get through the four barricaded entrances in the towering electric fence. Everyone else will be eyed up carefully. Dozens of private security guards will patrol the streets.

GEORGE: Today the first question is security. Like it or not, it's what makes the difference. When I grew up in London you had a community. You wouldn't do anything wrong because everyone knew you and they'd tell your mum and dad. You could play in the street and walk to school on your own. We want to re-create that here, a community which doesn't have to worry.

REPORTER: Heritage Park is designed as a self-contained community. Part of the site is given over to shops and small industries which the developer hopes will provide jobs to some residents. With schools, health clinics and work available inside the town, there should be no need to leave.

Those on the inside are not supposed to notice the electric fence around the town. They will be looking at the two salmon-filled lakes already set in what is planned as a 50-acre central park, or the stunning mountain views. For those who still want to leave its confines occasionally, Heritage Park is a mere 10 minutes' drive from the sea.

Mr Hazeldon came to South Africa on holiday from South London 24 years ago. He liked it so much that he never went back and became a South African citizen.

GEORGE: Anyone is welcome to live in Heritage Park, it doesn't matter what colour skin they have, the only criterion is that people want to live as good neighbours. We can build part of the 'Rainbow Nation' here.

REPORTER: But what about the thousand squatters living outside Heritage Park? They can't be forced to move. Well, Mr Hazeldon plans to build them a township of 142 houses in the far corner of the development. It will be on the outside of the electric fence but he hopes some of its residents will find work inside, in shops or as maids.

GEORGE: It's a win-win situation. They get free homes and we deal with an unsightly problem.

REPORTER: Mr Hazeldon plans to move to Heritage Park with his wife and two children. He's picked a prime site next to one of the lakes, a world away from South London. When Heritage Park is completed in ten years' time there will be 2000 homes.

7.7 A safe place to live?

Possible sentences to delete:

```
If we just look at health issues, it's
certain that more than half of the
population would not have survived various
diseases or medical conditions 200 years
ago.

People also died of shock after being
operated on without anaesthetic or from
infection afterwards.

Or soldiers might have arrested you and
forced you to join the army.    (56 fewer words)
```

8 Looking after yourself

8.1 Good health and illness

(Words not connected with this topic are in brackets)

Across: fit   bruise   disease   (*play*)   injection
(*wild*)   (*nice*)   cough   (*fun*)   (*easy*)   (*pair*)
diet   cure   faint   tablets   cuts   pain   pill
ache   sniff   nurse   (*set*)   fever   hurt
health   (*lot*)   temperature

Down: infection   drug   vaccine   sneeze
spot   medicine   (*neat*)   sick   bed

8.2 Modal verbs – 2

2 have been as difficult as
3 needn't/shouldn't have waited
4 should have woken up later / shouldn't have woken up so early   5 may have left
6 were able to swim   7 Did you (really) have/need to
8 couldn't sleep (a wink)

8.3 Hopi ear candles

2 E   3 D   4 G   5 A   6 C
(F doesn't fit anywhere)

8.4 Spelling and pronunciation – 2: Diphthongs

2 wear pair wore   3 wait mail   4 bread made
flour   5 waste fur sale   6 higher higher stairs
7 buy new   8 fair allowed

8.6 Poetry can cure you

1 B   2 B   3 C   4 A   5 A

T R A N S C R I P T *4 minutes*

INTERVIEWER: We all know that poetry is not everyone's cup of tea. But, according to Dr Jim Stewart…

DR STEWART: Hello.

INTERVIEWER: Hello…if you're suffering from anxiety or depression, poetry may be the solution to your problems. Dr Stewart, how does poetry help?

DR STEWART: Um…OK, look, let me give you an example. Um…a patient came into our clinic last month – and he was a middle-aged businessman and…he was feeling, well, like most middle-aged businessmen, really stressed and out of control of his life. And he talked to me about it and, well, I was convinced that medication just wouldn't help him. Then I read him a poem called *Leisure* by…er…WH Davies – um…do you know the one…er…it begins…um…

INTERVIEWER: I do, yes.

DR STEWART: "What is this life…er…so full of…" – is it 'so' or 'if'?

INTERVIEWER: No, I…I think it's 'if'.

DR STEWART: "… if full of care" – that's it, yes – "We have no time to stand and stare." – well, you know the one. The next time he came to me, he told me that, well, it was a sort of turning point for him. Er…the poem made him think about the quality of his life and the need to find a…a balance between his work and his social life. Um…you see, because the idea was expressed poetically, he felt that he could identify with it and actually feel the message in a way that…that he wouldn't if he'd simply discussed it with me and…er…and we'd just had a normal conversation about it.

INTERVIEWER: Yes, I see.

DR STEWART: You see, reading poetry to patients seems to make them calmer. Encouraging them to *write* it has an even more dramatic effect, actually. Er…there…there's something about the process of expressing confused thoughts…er…and feelings and emotions in writing that actually helps people who are suffering from stress or anxiety. Er…especially if the words are written in a poetic way, with a…with a sense of…er…sense of rhythm, rather than in prose, you see. Um…now, for a long time we've been asking patients to write diaries to put their feelings into words – but…um…it turns out that writing poetry seems to work much better for many patients.

INTERVIEWER: Right, and have you found that other doctors and therapists have made the same discoveries?

DR STEWART: Of…um…yes, many of my colleagues have successfully used poetry with patients suffering from…er…anxiety or depression – er…or even eating disorders.
I mean, their patients said that…that reading poetry made them feel less stressed. You know, a…almost as many said that writing it had the same effect. You see, some said that writing poetry reduced the pain they felt when a friend or…or close relation had died – extraordinary.

INTERVIEWER: Mm.

DR STEWART: Mm. Others thought that it…it enabled them to reduce or stop taking anti-depressants or tranquillisers. And writing poetry helps them to provide…um…a sort of outlet for their emotions.

INTERVIEWER: Mm, that's fascinating. Can you give any explanation as to why poetry might be calming in this way?

DR STEWART: Well, it's only a guess, I'd say that…that the calming effect of poetry is related to an interplay between the left and the right hemispheres of the brain. Er…you probably know the…the left one is the one which analyses and responds to language, the right one…er…visualises images and…er…and responds to rhythm. Now, I believe that poetry may activate the system at the base of the brain, where…um…where thoughts meet emotions. You see?

INTERVIEWER: Do…do you think that people need a doctor to prescribe particular poems for particular conditions?

DR STEWART: No, no. No, I think poetry can…er… help everyone to feel calm…and less stressed. People who read poetry tend not to be anxious and stressed – probably because they're in touch with their emotions. I mean, they certainly don't need a doctor to tell them which poems to read!

INTERVIEWER: Thank you very much, Dr Stewart.

DR STEWART: You're welcome.

8.8 Free life membership!

Two points missing from the letter:

• Why do you try to follow a healthy diet?

• How would joining the RENAISSANCE Club change your life?

9 Having a great time!

9.1 Travel and tourism

```
              17
 1  F  L  I  G  H  T
          2  A  G  E  N  T
          3  V  A  R  I  E  T  Y
 4  A  C  T  I  V  I  T  Y
 5  S  C  E  N  E  R  Y
 6  P  A  C  K  A  G  E
          7  S  E  A  S  I  D  E
          8  S  I  G  H  T  S
 9  E  X  C  U  R  S  I  O  N
       10  B  R  E  A  K  F  A  S  T
       11  C  H  A  R  T  E  R
12  S  U  N  B  A  T  H  E
          13  C  A  T  E  R  I  N  G
14  S  O  U  V  E  N  I  R
             15  M  O  U  N  T  A  I  N  S
16  B  R  O  C  H  U  R  E
```

9.2 Adventure holidays

	Nicaragua	Costa Rica	Neither
1	✓	✓	
2			✓
3	✓	✓	
4	✓	✓	
5	✓	✓	
6			✓
7	✓		
8	✓	✓	
9	✓		
10			✓
11	✓		
12	✓		
13	✓	✓	
14	✓		
15	✓	✓	

9.3 Spelling and pronunciation – 3: Consonants

A 2 accommodation 3 ✓ 4 whether
5 address 6 abbreviation 7 information
8 cheerfully 9 ✓ 10 collection

B millionaire immense assistant
(exhibition ✓) approximately whistle
knowledge secondary vehicle
(height ✓) fought doubled

9.4 *If . . .* sentences – 1

2 could afford it, I would 3 if you haven't got / if you don't have 4 I could swim I would be 5 in case it is/gets/turns 6 I were you I would 7 if I need any
8 had better book (ahead) if 9 until you reach
10 Would you prefer (to visit)

9.5 Paper 3: Use of English – Parts 1 and 2
Fill the gaps

(A)
1 B	2 B	3 B	4 D	5 B	6 B	7 B
8 A	9 D	10 C	11 A	12 B	13 D	
14 A	15 B					

(B)
16 about   17 who/that   18 than   19 good
20 should   21 wide/whole   22 kind/type/sort
23 with   24 for   25 gives   26 what
27 that/which   28 already   29 just   30 in

9.6 What went wrong?

1 C   2 D   3 F   4 E   5 B

TRANSCRIPT   *3 minutes 20 seconds*

SPEAKER 1 (MAN): Oh, it was a really bumpy flight and we were feeling pretty bad by the time we arrived. Er…by this time we were four hours late and it was nearly midnight. We had another couple of hours travelling ahead of us from the airport before we'd get to our hotel. Anyway we picked up our bags from the carousel, put them on a trolley and made our way to the station to get the train. It wasn't till we were on the train that we noticed a big hole in the side of one of the cases – and half the clothes inside were missing.

SPEAKER 2 (WOMAN): We had four cases between the two of us and it took a long time to get them into the taxi. It was the middle of the night and we'd phoned the hotel earlier that day to confirm our booking. So when we got there we unloaded the cases onto the pavement and paid the driver, who drove off. We rang the night bell at the hotel and the night porter opened the door – but there was no sign of our booking and there were no vacant rooms! We protested but there was nothing he could do. We'd sent the taxi away and we had four cases so we didn't know what to do.

SPEAKER 3 (MAN): We'd booked a family room with beds for the two kids. We had to carry our bags up to the room, which was on the fifth floor, because the lift wasn't working and the bell boy was on his lunch break, believe it or not! We opened up the door and couldn't believe our eyes. There was a double bed and two single beds, but they were all pushed together and there wasn't room for the four of us to stand up in the room at the same time. But it was the only room they had, they said.

SPEAKER 4 (WOMAN): It was very late by the time we got to the hotel. All we wanted to do was clean our teeth and go to bed. It took me ages to open the case because the key didn't seem to fit, but in the end I did. We had a quick wash and went to sleep straight away. The next morning I woke up and went to the window to open the blinds and go out onto the balcony to see what the weather was like. But, guess what? No sea? There was a nice view of the car park and the building opposite.

SPEAKER 5 (MAN): Er…we didn't get to the hotel till eight o'clock and we were afraid we might be too late for dinner but they went on serving till 8:30, so we decided to unpack later and dumped our case in the room and went straight to the restaurant. Er…after dinner – very nice – we went back upstairs and I got out my keys to unlock the case but…er…the key didn't seem to fit. The lock was jammed or something. Um…it was then that Jenny pointed out that the label on the case didn't have our name on it. It looked like our case, but it was…it was someone else's – we guessed they must have ours, very embarrassing!

9.7 A great holiday

Formal sentences which should be informal:

```
With reference to your letter of 15/9 I
should like to thank you for your kind
enquiries about my health.
→ Thanks for your letter, which I've
just re-read.

May I recommend that you follow the same
course of action next summer.
→ Why don't you go to Greece next
summer?

I look forward to your earliest reply,
→ Looking forward to hearing from you.
```

10 Food for thought

10.1 Foods and drinks

(The four drinks are underlined)

Across: salad   pasta   cucumber   vegetables   butter   meat   honey   pepper   potato   bread   cheese   beans   pie   rice   cream   salt   chocolate   tomato

Down: shrimp   fruit   beer   fish   egg   juice   apple   seafood   milk   tea   sauce

10.2 -*ing* and to … – 1

(A) 2 to eat/eating   3 eating   4 eating   5 to eat
6 to eat   7 eating   8 eating

(B) 2 rather have a salad than   3 looking forward to
4 worth cooking/preparing   5 Eating too much is bad
6 stopped eating   7 cheaper to eat at home
8 Squeezing a few oranges

10.3 Real cooking

1 A   2 C   3 C   4 C   5 B

10.4 Compound words – 1

(A) 2 -informed   3 -fashioned   -made
4 freshly-   juice   5 mineral   6 poisoning
7 opener   8 list   house

(B) 1 -aged   2 -control   3 -done   4 high-
5 floor   6 well-   7 -hearted   8 -footed

10.5 Five different situations

1 C   2 A   3 C   4 A   5 B

TRANSCRIPT   *2 minutes 30 seconds*

MAN: White wine or red?
WOMAN: I'd prefer red please.
MAN: Oh, I was hoping to have white.
WOMAN: Oh, why don't we have a glass of each?
MAN: Wine by the glass isn't a good idea, not here.
WOMAN: All right, I'll have water then.
MAN: Still or sparkling?
WOMAN: Still.
MAN: In that case we might as well have a jug of ordinary water. No point in paying for a bottle.
WOMAN: All right.

WAITRESS: Your bill, sir.
MAN: Thank you. …Oh, that's seems a lot.
WOMAN: Let's see. Oh, yes. How much was the wine?
MAN: £10.

WOMAN: They've charged us for two. We only had one.
MAN: That's right. Er…how much was the total again?
WOMAN: No, £46. So with one bottle of wine less that's…
MAN: Er…and is service included?
WOMAN: No, we need to add about ten per cent.
MAN: Well, let's make it £4, round it up.

WOMAN: So that's about everything we can do at this stage before everyone arrives.
MAN: What about the salad?
WOMAN: Oh, there's no point in putting the dressing on yet.
MAN: But we could prepare the dressing now.
WOMAN: All right. You can do that now.
MAN: I'd rather you did it, your dressing is always better than mine.
WOMAN: Oh, let's wait till Dick gets here – we can ask him to make his famous dressing.
MAN: Oh, yes. He'll like that!

MAN: I feel like a nice dessert tonight.
WOMAN: Apple and blackberry pie?
MAN: Ooh, that's a good idea.
WOMAN: We've still got some blackberries in the freezer.
MAN: And there's plenty of apples. I'll peel them.
WOMAN: Ah, there's a problem, I think.
MAN: What's that?
WOMAN: There doesn't seem to be any flour or sugar.
MAN: Are you sure?
WOMAN: Oh, no, just a minute there's some flour here. But only flour.

TIM: OK, how are we going to do this?
ANNE: We all had more or less the same. So why don't we just divide it all by three and each pay our share?
BOB: No, no, no, it's my birthday and I invited you and Tim, so I should pay.
ANNE: Oh, no, that's not fair. Tim, let's make it our treat. Let's split the bill between the two of us.
TIM: Um…sorry Anne, the problem is I haven't quite got enough cash on me, and they don't take credit cards here.
ANNE: Don't they? Oh, dear, I didn't realize that. Oh, how embarrassing! Sorry, Bob.
BOB: OK, luckily I went to a cash machine on the way here.

10.6 Prepositions

2 went past   3 came towards / came up to
4 instead of   5 ran away from the dog
6 was delayed owing to   7 the plate on purpose
8 By the time you arrive   9 at the same time
10 met by chance

10.7 Verbs and idioms

2 make out   3 make one up
4 get on (well) with / get along (well) with
5 look it up   6 could (really) do with
7 he was getting at   8 see you off at
9 gave up trying   10 given back

10.9 A birthday celebration

The two irrelevant sentences are:

We can't be there before then because we have to attend an extra evening lesson at school.

The reason for this is that some of our group have a very limited budget and just can't manage £12 for a meal.

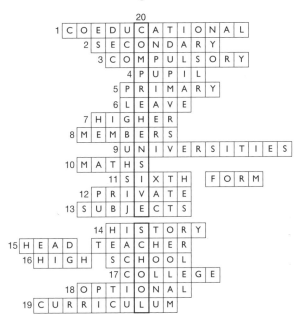

11 You never stop learning

11.1 Schools and colleges

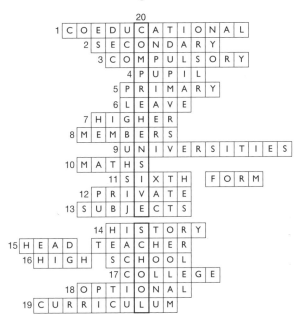

11.2 How to do well in exams

2 C   3 B   4 E   5 A   6 H
7 D   (G doesn't fit anywhere)

11.3 If … sentences – 2

A 2 unless you give me the   3 would have stayed/kept dry if   4 in case it gets/becomes   5 had not been delayed / had not been late   6 get on well because

B 2 were you I'd try to/and   3 hadn't met her there, I wouldn't have been/felt (so)   4 have time I hope to be able to / have time I hope I will be able to   5 had finished (my) supper in time I would/might have gone 6 had driven more carefully he wouldn't have had

11.4 Compound words – 2

A 1 -sighted   2 second- brand-   3 account/bank
4 playing/football   5 -looking   6 -minute

B 1 timetable   2 toothache   3 notebook
4 airports   5 schoolgirl   6 postmen/postgraduates

11.5 Paper 3: Use of English – Part 4 Correcting errors

1 ✓   2 ✓   3 out   4 the   5 the   6 has
7 ✓   8 ✓   9 this   10 even   11 was
12 the   13 ✓   14 then   15 out

11.6 Co-educational or single-sex schools?

Composition separated into paragraphs.

Many schoolboys are noisy and badly-behaved. They disturb the class and destroy the concentration of the other pupils. The reasons for this type of behaviour is because they are trying to impress each other with their disregard for authority or when they are older because they want to show off to the girls.

    Having boys in the class can adversely affect girls' learning. They don't ask questions and don't get the teacher's attention. In a single-sex environment, girls compete with each other and want to be top but mixed with boys they don't want to appear competitive or clever.

On the other hand, boys and girls educated together socialise on a daily basis and thus have more realistic expectations of each other.

Generally, it is better for boys to be educated with girls but not so good for girls.

12 What shall we do this evening?

12.1 Entertainment

Across: game show rock cable TV news director film award star western video cartoon

Down: cinema dubbed thriller channel music romantic Oscar jazz horror comedy documentary actor crime

12.2 -ing and to ... – 2

1 couldn't help laughing when   2 refused to help
3 didn't remember to   4 stop talking because
5 me to help her (to)   6 went on running
7 is very/really good at (playing)   8 interested in finding out

12.3 Which film ...?

1 and 2 A B   3 E   4 C   5 C   6 and 7 A D
8 and 9 E F   10 A   11 F   12 and 13 A B
14 C

12.4 Using suffixes – 1: Adjectives

A

childish/childless   foggy
accidental   historical   delightful
successful   regional   forgetful
educational   painful/painless   hopeful/hopeless

B

1 uncomfortable   2 jobless   3 fashionable
4 speechless   5 draughty   6 unreliable
7 admirable   8 tactless

12.5 What did you think of it?

1 A   2 B   3 C   4 B   5 A

TRANSCRIPT *3 minutes*

MAN: Did you enjoy it?
WOMAN: Not really. I thought it was rather disappointing.
MAN: Oh, why's that?
WOMAN: It wasn't really what I expected. It went on too long.
MAN: No, but...but you must admit that on the big screen it looked great.
WOMAN: Well, I think it would have been just as good seeing it at home.
MAN: Ah, but it won't even be on video till next year.
WOMAN: I could have waited that long.

WOMAN: What are you doing this evening?
MAN: Well, I've got a lot of work to do, I ought to stay at home and study really.
WOMAN: Oh, come on, it's Saturday.
MAN: Well, how about going to the cinema, then?
WOMAN: There's nothing on that I want to see.
MAN: Oh, all right, well, we could rent a video and watch that.
WOMAN: But neither of us has got a video recorder.
MAN: No, but Tony's got a new DVD player. How about

renting a movie to watch with him at his place?
WOMAN: Oh, that's a great idea!
MAN: That was really good, wasn't it?
WOMAN: Yeah, where does the pianist come from?
MAN: Russia, I think. She was terrific.
WOMAN: Pity about the audience though.
MAN: Yeah, I know. It always happens in the quiet bits.
WOMAN: Coughing is bad enough.
MAN: But that wasn't so bad today.
WOMAN: People forget to turn them off, that's the trouble.
MAN: You know, I don't think they should be allowed to even bring them into the building.
WOMAN: Oh, that's a bit extreme. It's OK out here in the bar. Which reminds me, I promised to call Bill. Excuse me a moment...
MAN: Problem?
WOMAN: Yes, we'll have to change our plans.
MAN: I told you it would be popular.
WOMAN: That's not the problem. We should have checked the paper before we set off.
MAN: But Alex saw it yesterday – he said it started at 8 and it's ten to now. So what's the problem?
WOMAN: Well, Alex must have seen the special preview. That was yesterday. The woman told me that it's not on general release till next week.
MAN: Oh, is there something else you'd like to see? The new James Bond maybe?
WOMAN: I don't think so.

FRANK: Ohh, thank goodness that's over!
LIZ: Oh, yes, what a bore!
TONY: Frank, you're the one who persuaded us to go.
FRANK: Sorry, Tony. Sorry, Liz.
LIZ: Well, at least the costumes were good. I quite liked the lighting, didn't you, Tony?
TONY: The lighting? I didn't even notice it. But the dancing was OK, I suppose. Frank you're the expert on dance, did you think it was reasonably OK?
FRANK: I didn't even think the music was any good.
LIZ and The *music* wasn't too bad!
TONY:

12.6 Paper 3: Use of English – Part 3 Rewriting sentences

31 wish I had gone
32 would like to know
33 gave up trying to phone/call/ring
34 told/ordered us not to make
35 had better send (them)
36 have been friends since
37 is hardly ever
38 too expensive (for me)
39 if I hadn't/had not read
40 eat as many vegetables as

12.8 I'm sorry you missed the end ...

Second paragraph split into shorter sentences:

After you left, the scene moved to Europe but we weren't sure where because there was no dialogue for ages. It was very unclear. But it turned out to be Italy, where the heroine was studying to be a doctor. She was working as housekeeper for a pianist and she also had a room in his house, which was full of the sound of classical music.

13 Read any good books?

13.1 Books and magazines

```
          18
 1 S T O R Y
       2 C O N T E N T S
   3 B L U R B
   4 T H R I L L E R
           5 F I C T I O N
 6 L I T E R A T U R E
       7 R E V I E W
       8 P L O T
         9 A U T H O R
10 C H A R A C T E R S
     11 L I B R A R Y
  12 T I T L E
     13 L E N D
             14 B I O G R A P H Y
  15 G L O S S A R Y
       16 C O V E R
17 B O O K S H O P
```

13.2 When do you read?

1 E   2 F   3 D   4 C   5 A

TRANSCRIPT *2 minutes 20 seconds*

SPEAKER 1 (MAN): I must confess I'm not much of a reader. There was a time when I read all the time, but I find I'm so busy now that I hardly ever open a book. Except during holidays – that's the time I catch up on my reading. I get through a book a day then. I like John le Carré very much.

SPEAKER 2 (WOMAN): I read quite a lot, um…mainly modern novels and bestsellers. I've tried setting aside an hour a day to read during the day in the living room, or…um…in the garden if it's warm, but there are always interruptions. For me the best place to read is tucked up under the covers with my feet up before I go to sleep. I read every evening and…er…my favourite writer is John Grisham.

SPEAKER 3 (MAN): By the time it's bedtime I'm too tired to read. No, the best time for me is mornings and evenings. I commute to work by rail and the journey takes an hour. So I don't make calls on my mobile or catch up on my office work, I take a book and just enter a different world. My favourite author is Barbara Vine.

SPEAKER 4 (WOMAN): I read a lot actually. Magazines, newspapers, reports, things like that. But one of the things I regret is that although I did read a lot of books during my schooldays, I haven't read a single one since then. Do you know, I think the last one I read was *The Great Gatsby*. Terrible, isn't it?

SPEAKER 5 (MAN): My wife always reads in bed before we put the lights out and…er…I used to do so too. But lately, when I do open a book, I just find myself dropping off before I've even finished a page. I never suffer from insomnia – but it takes a very long time to get through a book.

13.3 Joining sentences – 1: Relative clauses

1   who phoned and asked for you spoke with a foreign accent.
2   , who also writes under the name Barbara Vine, writes crime stories.
3   , who is a millionaire, is the main character in the book.
4   , whose real name is David Cornwell, writes spy stories.
5   , who used to be a hospital doctor, wrote *Jurassic Park*.
6   , who was a lawyer before he became a writer, is one of the world's best-selling authors.
7   John le Carré wrote *The Night Manager*, which is about a man who works in a hotel.
8   books (that/which) I particularly enjoy reading are thrillers.

13.4 Using suffixes – 2: Actions and people

A participant   guitarist   narrator   employer
observer   photographer   novelist   assistant
pianist   supervisor   inventor

B 1 sweetened   2 terrified   3 criticised/criticized
4 brightened   5 generalising/generalizing
6 widened   7 visitors   8 biologist

13.5 Cambridge English Readers

1 D   2 E   3 C   4 A   5 B
(F doesn't fit anywhere)

1 A   2 C   3 D (not B)   4 H   5 E
6 G (not F)   7 L   8 I   9 J (not K)   10 O
11 N   12 M (not P)

14 All in a day's work

14.1 Jobs and employment

Across: staff   profit   training   email   apply
profession   factory   department   interview
office   fire   sack   manager   pension
employee   boss   retire

Down: salary   wages   firm   job   rise
career   promotion   employer

14.2 Joining sentences – 2: Conjunctions

1 such a bad trip/journey that
2 although she had a terrible
3 haven't played cards since   4 so that I would/could
5 despite feeling (very) nervous / despite his nervousness
6 after losing his / after he had lost his
7 even though she was   8 so happy about/after

14.3 At Last I Have Time!

1 D   2 E   3 C   4 E   5 B   6 A   7 D
8 D   9 A   10 D

14.4 Using suffixes – 3: Abstract nouns

A efficiency   simplicity
ability   shyness
patience   generosity
pride   boredom
frequency   anxiety
arrogance   hunger
brilliance   thirst

B 1 pronunciation   2 explanations   3 retirement
4 disapproval   5 survival   6 imagination
7 entertainment   8 arrivals   departures

14.5 Having fun at work

1 creativity   2 five years ago   3 seriously
4 blame each other (for mistakes) / don't trust each other
5 everyone   6 large / older / a more traditional
7 trust   8 think (about what they're doing)
9 pressure   10 knowledge   11 customer services
12 loses

TRANSCRIPT *3 minutes 40 seconds*

PRESENTER: Do you enjoy your work? Is it fun? A recent report compares companies where the workers are having fun with companies where the workers are miserable. Tony Davies reports. Tony.

REPORTER: Yes, thanks, Sally. Now, this report clearly suggests that in a workplace where there's an atmosphere of playfulness, and laughter and humour – like ours! – there is a significant improvement in activities which are innovative and creative. In other words, having fun leads to creativity.

The report also found, conversely, that work places where the employees are under a lot of pressure and where there are high levels of stress, creativity doesn't flourish.

In the financial services sector, for example, some of the current winners are clearly those that have focused on innovation. Richard Branson's Virgin Group has become one of the leading savings, investment and loan groups – er…the group only started five years ago from nothing. Branson himself sets perhaps the clearest example among company heads for someone who really enjoys life, doesn't take himself too seriously and…er…basically likes a joke. This is evident from his famous hot air ballooning, um…his beard, his informal dress (he never wears a suit and tie), er…the staff parties thrown at his house, and his habit of dressing up in silly clothing!

The report finds that creativity is unlikely to flourish in an organisation where people blame each other for mistakes. Now, some companies try to develop élite creativity units, by putting together a committee or group of imaginative people, but that's actually a big mistake. They will usually be less successful than those who bring in everyone in the company, including the maintenance man and the receptionist. Everyone has to be part of the process, because they all have ideas to contribute.

But being radically creative in a traditional, unquestioning environment has serious dangers. If you work in an insurance company that has done things the same way for 150 years you could get yourself fired if you start to talk about making big changes. If you want to be creative, you have to find the right sort of company to work in. Creative companies tend to be smaller, new ones rather than big, traditional industries.

The problem is that a lot of companies are restricting both the thinking time of their employees and their opportunities for creativity. You see, something like creativity will usually only flourish where there's an atmosphere of trust. Also people have to have enough time to think about what they're doing. If you're always under pressure, always working to tight deadlines, and if your boss is breathing down your neck all the time and doesn't trust you, you can't have fun – and that means you can't usually be creative.

PRESENTER: All right, but why is creativity important? Surely most workers don't need to be creative.

REPORTER: Well, i…in the days when a worker's role was to be…um…a human part of the machinery on a production line, an individual's creativity was hardly a commercial issue. But now, in a world where a company's economic edge comes from knowledge and customer service rather than physical muscle and power, the development of creativity will, I think you'll find, increasingly separate the winning companies from…er…well, from the losers.

14.7   A summer job

Irrelevant information:

Working with children + working as a waiter
Playing the piano

Missing information:

Age   Languages he speaks

15 Can you explain?

15.1   Technology and science

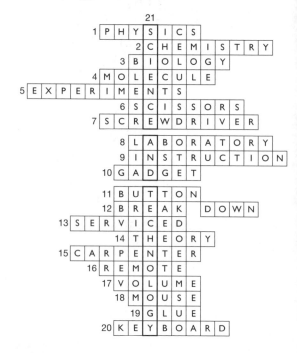

15.2   The Swiss Army Knife

1 D   2 C   3 B   4 G   5 H
6 E   7 A   (F doesn't fit anywhere, but it is true)

15.3   Using the passive

1 was invented   2 was taking   3 found
4 were covered   5 made   6 attached
7 were examined   8 observed   9 were covered
10 had become   11 was born   12 have made
13 ran   14 was attempted   15 came
16 was sewn   17 were created   18 was made
19 came   20 be used   21 is used   22 throws
23 gets   24 plunges

15.4   Opposites

A   noisy/loud   inaccurate   shy/diffident
rude/impolite   stale   full
dangerous/unsafe   cheap/inexpensive

B   lie   turn off   oppose
lose   fail   begin/start
lose   accept   mend/repair/fix

15.5   Paper 4: Listening – Parts 1 and 2

1 B   2 A   3 C   4 A   5 B   6 C
7 C   8 B

TRANSCRIPT *5 minutes 30 seconds*

MAN: What do you think of it?
WOMAN: Very nice. I like the colour.
MAN: Haha. It goes like a rocket.
WOMAN: I'll bet it does. The seat looks a bit uncomfortable though.
MAN: Yes, it took a bit of getting used to.
WOMAN: Is it expensive to run?
MAN: No, I only have to fill it up once a week.
WOMAN: But it can't be very nice in wet weather.

MAN: Oh, it's got a roof. It folds out from here, look.
WOMAN: Oh, that's neat.

MAN: Here you have a go.
WOMAN: Oh, I hate these things.
MAN: No, go on. Press the forward arrow button.
WOMAN: Oh, yes, I see, that makes it start.
MAN: And now press the red one.
WOMAN: All right. Oh, it's stopped. And the TV's gone off too.
MAN: That's right. It controls both of them. This replaces them both.
WOMAN: Two for the price of one?
MAN: Yeah, and it was only £10.

WOMAN: When I drive off it works fine but after about 20 minutes it just stops working. Yes, I have checked the connections. No, what happens then is, I leave the car parked for a while, start off again and the radio works again for 20 minutes then it goes off. The problem is if someone comes round to look at it it'll probably be working fine. He could sit in the car with me while I drive around for 20 minutes, but he may not want to do that. So can you ask him what I should do please?

MAN: How much money did you put in?
WOMAN: A two-pound coin.
MAN: But nothing came out?
WOMAN: No. But the display here said "Thank you" when I put the coin in and then it said "Please wait for your change".
MAN: I see, yeah. That's funny because it's never happened before. Well, I can't really do anything about it. But I can give you a card to write your complaint on and you can post it in the complaints box over there.
WOMAN: But I want to go to Piccadilly Circus and that was the only change I had. And the window's closed, so I have to use one of the machines. The only money I have is a £10 note.
MAN: I can give you change for £10 and you could try one of the other machines.

MAN: You won't believe this!
WOMAN: What happened?
MAN: Well, there was a sign outside saying "Back in five minutes" so I waited outside for about 10 minutes. Then he opened the door from the inside! He didn't say he was sorry or anything, just let me in. I put the video on the counter and I spent five minutes explaining what had gone wrong, and showed him the guarantee which he looked at carefully. And you'll never guess what he said: "Can you come back tomorrow? I don't feel very well today." Imagine that!

WOMAN: How much is it?
MAN: Er…£599 plus VAT.
WOMAN: So that's just over £700.
MAN: Mm. Look at the specifications – it's pretty impressive, eh?
WOMAN: Yes, I'll take your word for that, and it looks really nice too.
MAN: Er…I'd really like to have one, wouldn't you?
WOMAN: Yes, I'd use it all the time if I did.
MAN: The problem is that they can't ship them for six months.
WOMAN: Are they taking advance orders?
MAN: No.
WOMAN: Well, that's it then.

MAN: And if you'd just like to come this way I can show you something else that will interest you. Look at this!
TWO PEOPLE: Oh! Mm.
MAN: Yes, it's pretty impressive, isn't it. When this one first came out it cost a fortune, but now it's nowhere near as expensive – and it's a thousand times more powerful too. This one on the left is the original model – it looks really old-fashioned now, doesn't it?

MAN: Right, there we are. All fixed.
WOMAN: All right. Thank you. Are you sure it's going to be OK?
MAN: Oh, yes, good for another five years now.
WOMAN: Oh. So I won't be needing one of those lovely new ones, then? I was looking at them in town the other day. They are more reliable than the old model, I suppose.
MAN: Haha, not really, they all break down from time to time.
WOMAN: Oh, well, thank you. I'll call you if it goes wrong again.

B   9 nuclear attack   10 central control   11 types
12 packets   13 clients   14 server   15 routers
16 Geneva, Switzerland   17 (January) 1992
18 When it's morning in America / when Americans are checking their e-mails in the mornings.

TRANSCRIPT   *4 minutes 20 seconds*

PRESENTER: We all take the Internet for granted now, but how did it all start? Jill Drake has been looking at the history of the Net. Jill.
REPORTER: Well, back in 1966 computers couldn't talk to each other. That's why an organization in the USA called Advanced Research Projects Agency (ARPA for short – it was the Pentagon's research and development unit) set up a network so that its staff in different parts of the USA could exchange messages through their computers. They designed a computer network that could still function as a network, even if it was partially destroyed by a nuclear attack. The network was called the ARPANET and it was the forerunner of the modern Internet. It was based on two important principles: first, it was just a distribution system which had no central control, and second it could connect computers of different types. The computers were linked by normal phone lines. Each computer had a modem which translated digital signals into the analogue signals that all telephone systems used at that time.
    This small network grew as more non-military research institutions joined in. This led in 1983 to the development of the Internet, which is based on something called Internet Protocol (or IP). IP is a system which decides how a message is split into small packets of data. Each packet can be sent by a different route to the destination, and the IP reassembles the packets into a complete message at the other end. Each message is split into packets to be transmitted – this uses the phone lines much more efficiently than a continuous stream of data and enables much more data to be sent on the same line. At this time the network was mainly used by staff and students in universities to send e-mail messages to each other, not so much by members of the public.
PRESENTER: What are Servers and Routers?
REPORTER: Well, these are powerful computers which are the engines that make the system work. Across the world individual users or 'clients' send messages to a Server – a powerful computer that organises the splitting of packets of data and decides when and where to send them. Most companies and universities have their own Servers, individuals use the server of their ISP – that's Internet Service Provider. The Internet is not a single network, it's an international web of interconnected government, education, and business computer networks – a network of networks. These networks are connected by powerful computers known as Routers. Your computer is told the location of its nearest router when you dial into your ISP or to your Server – and sends packets to it.
    Routers across the world forward these packets down their attached phone lines, satellite links or other networks to another router in the general direction of a packet's destination.
PRESENTER: What about the World Wide Web?
REPORTER: Well, the development of the World Wide Web was begun in 1989 by Tim Berners-Lee and his

colleagues at CERN, this is the international scientific organization based in Geneva, Switzerland. They created a system called HyperText Transfer Protocol (HTTP), which standardized communication between servers and clients. The first Web browser was made available for general release in January 1992. Within a few years everyone with a computer was on line – surfing the World Wide Web and sending e-mails to each other.

PRESENTER: Now, a few years ago people were saying that the whole system would slow down to a stop because so much information was being sent down so few phone lines. Is that going to happen?

REPORTER: Mm, well, at certain times of day, as we all know, things do slow down. The time to avoid going on line is when America is waking up. Every computer user in America checks their e-mails in the morning. But better and better methods of compressing data are being developed, so that less band width is needed. Also telephone companies encourage Internet traffic (because they make most of their money from it), so it's in their interest to keep pace with demand by providing enough phone lines, satellite links and cables.

PRESENTER: But the longer you spend on line the more you pay the phone company. So maybe it's in their interest to keep you waiting?

15.6 Prepositions

1 confidence   2 tears   3 apologised/apologized
4 consists   5 relying/depending   6 revising
7 suffering   8 pay   9 tired   10 insisted
capable   11 Congratulations   12 succeeded

15.7 What can go wrong?

Spelling mistakes:

brakes up → breaks up   restrat → restart
certin → certain

16 Keeping up to date

16.1 In the news

Across: news   editorial   headline   report
murder   cartoon   jail   disaster   documentary
column   government   robbery   leader
election   parliament   refugees

Down: reporter   article   trial   crime   story
president   war   photo

16.2 The past – 3: Reported speech

1 asked me to help   2 claimed (that) he couldn't
3 (that) he had committed / having committed
4 advised me to check my / advised checking my
5 asked me if I was   6 I wasn't/was not using
7 know when the film began/started   8 was doing on
Friday / was doing that day   9 would come when he
had   10 to ring him on Sunday

16.3 Paper 1: Reading – Part 4

B   1 D   2 C   3 A   4 B   5 A   6 C   7 B
8 B   9 D   10 B   11 B   12 C   13 D
14 B

16.4 Paper 4: Listening – Parts 3 and 4

A   19 C   20 E   21 F   22 A   23 D
(nobody said B)

TRANSCRIPT *2 minutes 40 seconds*

SPEAKER 1 (MAN): This burglar robbed a big house in the suburbs. He got away with the video and jewellery and cash. But while he was in the house he found a camera and for a joke he took a photo of himself with it. And then, hearing a noise he dropped the camera and got away quickly. The woman who owned the house didn't know about the camera until she'd finished the film and had it developed three months afterwards. Among the photos was a picture of the man: the police picked him up the same day!

SPEAKER 2 (WOMAN): A burglar broke into a flat and started collecting up all the valuables. Among the things was a Polaroid camera. He took two photos of himself in a mirror with the camera but when blank sheets came out, well, he thought it wasn't working properly, so he left the camera behind. The next morning the police found the photos, recognised the man and found him at home with all the stuff he had taken from the flat.

SPEAKER 3 (MAN): This soldier was really short of money and decided to rob a bank. He had it all planned out and went in there with a gun and wearing a stocking mask over his face so that nobody could recognise him. Unfortunately for him, he was still wearing his military uniform, complete with name tag.

SPEAKER 4 (WOMAN): This bank robber fell over the doormat as he ran into the bank. And as he fell, his mask slipped from his face and his gun went off. Then he got up but slipped again on the floor, which had just been washed, and dropped his gun. By this time, the bank staff and customers were laughing so much that he just decided to run away empty-handed. He ran out of the bank and crashed into a policeman, who was writing a parking ticket for his car, which he he'd just left outside the bank.

SPEAKER 5 (MAN): Another bank robber was caught on video. Instead of wearing a mask or a…a stocking, he wore a pair of tights on his head. He looked so stupid with the legs of the tights hanging down the sides of his face – like a rabbit with floppy ears – that the police were sure they'd catch him pretty soon. But he had the last laugh.

B   24 C   25 B   26 B   27 C   28 C
29 B   30 A

TRANSCRIPT *3 minutes*

PRESENTER: Another unusual Atlantic crossing ended happily today when four artists too poor to fly but keen to see the world crossed the Atlantic with three dogs aboard a boat called 'The Son of Town Hall'. Landing on Ireland's west coast yesterday, their skipper said they were 'only slightly insane'. Kate Williams is there now.

REPORTER: Villagers at Castletownbere, Co Cork, were not so sure. They described the vessels as 'a garden shed', a doll's house', 'a rubbish tip' and 'a lunatic asylum'. Edward Garry is the captain. Ed, how long did the voyage take?

ED GARRY: We set off from Halifax, Nova Scotia, 63 days ago in our sail and engine the sail and engine-powered craft, 'The Son of Town Hall'. We had to dodge icebergs, storms and 25-foot waves.

REPORTER: It doesn't look like any boat I've ever seen. What is it made out of?

ED GARRY: It's a composite of recycled materials, scrap metal and discarded wood. And we have put it together to make our dreams come true. We set out for France, but when we saw Ireland in our vision, we decided to go for it. I am going to have a shower and a pint and meet the beautiful people of Ireland. We are all a little crazy in our own way – I just demonstrate it a little more pointedly.

REPORTER: And how many of you are there on board?

ED GARRY: Er...the crew consists of Poppino Neutrino and his wife, Aurelia – they're a married couple in their 60s from San Francisco – Roger Doncaster, a Canadian, and me – I'm an Irish-American. The dogs are two Rottweilers, Siegfried and Thor, and a Mexican poodle called Willie. We all, humans and dogs, lived on pasta and tinned food.

REPORTER: The Irish coastguard said that you were in serious danger and were very lucky that the weather was calm.

ED GARRY: Mm, I didn't feel in danger at any stage. We had sails and an engine and they worked perfectly. I never had any doubt that we would make it. We had all the necessary safety equipment: a VHF radio, two megaband transceivers and flares. The boat was coastguard-approved before we set off and is completely seaworthy. It just looks a little funny. The only problem was that our supplies were running low because we expected the 3,000-mile journey to last 30 days, not 63. An Irish naval ship, the LE Eimear, resupplied us on Tuesday when we entered Irish waters. The dogs aren't going to set paw on land because if they do they'll have to go into quarantine for six months. We're staying in Ireland for two weeks.

REPORTER: So where are you going next?

ED GARRY: We're going to sail around the Mediterranean!

16.6 A letter to the editor

Mistakes with Capital letters:

Dear sir → Dear Sir   the main story → The main story
I like To read → I like to read

17 It's a small world

17.1 Countries, cities and nationalities

17.2 Paper 1: Reading – Part 3

1 I   2 C   3 E   4 J   5 B   6 H   7 F
8 A   (G doesn't fit anywhere)

17.3 Comparing and contrasting

1 as many inhabitants as   2 is bigger than
3 is the second largest/biggest country
4 has fewer mountains than   5 twice as many people as
6 is half the size of   7 is less mountainous than
8 as much rainforest as   9 is (quite/fairly) similar to
10 is much more dangerous than / much less safe than

17.4 Paper 3: Use of English – Part 5 Word formation

B 1 cultural   2 Unfortunately   3 majority
4 inhabitants   5 attraction/attractions   6 seaside
7 preparations   8 thoroughly   9 Surprisingly
10 knowledge

17.5 Local customs

1 C   2 F   3 A   4 B   5 E   (nobody said D)

TRANSCRIPT   3 minutes 45 seconds

SPEAKER 1 (MAN): It was my first visit to Germany and I'd been to language classes before I went, so I could speak the language quite well. I was there for six months and attending classes at university. But I was finding it very hard to make friends. Whenever I spoke to people they gave me a funny look and were a bit cold. Then someone took me aside and explained that I was speaking in a too formal way to everyone, using 'Sie' as I'd been told. Apparently students use 'du' with each other, even if they don't know each other well. I thought 'du' was only used when you've become close friends. So I was giving everyone the wrong impression.

SPEAKER 2 (WOMAN): I thought I knew all about the USA when I went there. I'd seen so many movies and TV shows. I really enjoyed myself and soon became accustomed to the way people behaved. There was just one thing that was still strange after two months. Everyone cuts up their food into bite-sized pieces using their knife and fork in the normal way. Then they put the knife down, pick up the fork with their right hand and put all the food in their mouths with the fork. Very strange!

SPEAKER 3 (MAN): I was staying with a family in France and they were really nice. The food was terrific – we had a huge lunch every day and I found it hard to keep going in the afternoon, I was so full up. But what I couldn't get used to was this: whenever people came to the house or we went out to meet people, all the women and girls expected me to touch cheeks and kiss the air. I could never work out which cheek to touch first and how many times to do it. I could feel myself blushing every time this happened because I felt uncomfortable about having to do this. But I was younger then, so I'd probably not feel the same now.

SPEAKER 4 (WOMAN): When I went to Spain for the first time, I stayed with a family. They were really nice and...er...they...they took me all over on visits to...er...places and out for meals. But what was strange to me was that they had their meals so late. If we went out to eat we didn't go to the restaurant till 10 pm – I was feeling quite tired by then and I was also starving. In the end I bought myself some chocolate bars and had a secret snack at 5 o'clock!

SPEAKER 5 (MAN): I'd been to Germany lots of times but this had never happened to me before. I was in a little town, staying with some friends. Er...I hadn't had any lunch and I was on my way to meet my friends for coffee and cakes in the afternoon. The traffic lights were red for pedestrians but there was no traffic coming so I started to cross. Then this woman started shouting at me. She told me off for crossing against the lights and said I was lucky there wasn't a policeman watching or else I'd've got fined!

17.7 Paper 2: Writing – Part 2

Spelling mistakes:

payed → paid   approching → approaching
raelly → really

18 Yes, but is it art?

18.1 Art and music

Across: dramatist   composer   solo   painting
potter   violin   rock   orchestra   stage
genius   portrait

Down: arts   surrealist   opera   sculpture   rap
piano   jazz   band   actor   pop   conductor
abstract   singer   theatre   landscape

18.2 The future

1 your/the train arrives   2 will already have closed/
shut/will already be closed/shut   3 wife is going to have
4 am going to pick my friend up   5 shall/should/can we
get   6 arrive the lesson will be   7 be doing while I
am   8 should/can/shall I come round
9 (probably) won't begin work/working
10 am going (away/off) on holiday

18.3 Paper 1: Reading – Part 1

1 H   2 J   3 C   4 B   5 I   6 E   7 A
8 F   (D doesn't fit anywhere)

18.4 The next day ...

1 13   2 seaside resort   3 sunlamps   4 Customs
5 arrivals screen   6 film   7 its money back
8 challenges

TRANSCRIPT   *2 minutes 30 seconds*

PRESENTER: National newspapers reported yesterday about the
art students in Leeds who raised £1600 from
sponsors and spent it all on a holiday in Spain. Well,
it seems that we were all being taken for a ride. Ray
Brown reports. Ray.

RAY: That's right, Fiona. The students held a press
conference this morning and revealed that they had
never left England.
The 13 students are the entire third year on a
Fine Arts course at Leeds University, and they now
say said that the whole thing was an elaborate hoax.
Yesterday, as you know, the students released
photographs which seemed to show them on the
beach on the Costa del Sol. But now it seems that
the photos were taken in Scarborough (the nearest
seaside resort to Leeds), and others were shot in
pubs in Leeds and next to a swimming pool in
Bromley, Kent.
The people who came to the opening of an
exhibition, 'Going Places', were taken by bus to
Leeds–Bradford Airport and there they met the 13
suntanned students arriving through Customs saying
they had used the money intended for the
exhibition for a week's holiday. The suntans were
acquired by spending hours under sunlamps. The
arrival through Customs was provided with the help
of the management of Leeds–Bradford Airport.
Leeds–Bradford Airport confirmed that it agreed
to allow the students to appear as if they were
coming through the Arrivals doors. They also put a
fake announcement on the flight arrivals screen for
a non-existent flight from Malaga. The students said
that they were making a film for their degree course
and this was one of the scenes from the film.

Leeds Students' Union were one of the sponsors.
Their communications officer says that people are
quite angry and this makes students seem a bit of a
joke. The Union still wants its money back.
The students say that the stunt challenges the
boundaries of art. If art is a way of making people
reflect on life and provoking discussion, then what
they did succeeded in doing this. It also generated a
lot of publicity, which was good for the University
and for the Fine Art Department, they claim.

PRESENTER: Hmm, any publicity is good publicity, as they say.
Thank you, Ray.

18.6 An exhibition

Letter divided into paragraphs:

```
I am writing to tell you about an
exhibition at the Serpentine Gallery that
you won't want to miss. It's a Bridget
Riley show, her paintings from the 1960s
and 70s. I know you love her work. So why
don't we combine a visit to the exhibition
with lunch and the chance to spend the day
together.

I know it's a long way to come for a day
but the exhibition is free and there's a
special offer on the trains. If you get a
day return on any Saturday in July, the
fare is only £39, which is less than half
the price of the normal fare. However, you
must book it in advance.

I've checked on the trains and there are
several that would get you into King's
Cross before midday. I think the 07.30
from Newcastle arriving at 10.38 would be
the best.

Please write and let me know if you're
interested and if so which train you will
be getting. I'll meet you at King's Cross.

Look forward to hearing from you,
```

19 Other people

19.1 Personality and behaviour

```
                    17
1  R O M A N T I C
2  N A U G H T Y
        3  J E A L O U S
4  R E L I A B L E
   5  L I K E A B L E
   6  S E N S I T I V E
7  B A D - T E M P E R E D
      8  L O Y A L
   9  S E L F I S H
10 C H E E R F U L
   11 W A R M - H E A R T E D
      12 W I T T Y
      13 S E R I O U S
      14 G E N E R O U S
15 C O N F I D E N T
      16 S H Y
```

19.2 Paper 1: Reading – Part 2

1 C   2 B   3 C   4 B   5 D   6 D
7 A   8 D

19.3   Adverbs and word order

1 hardly ever speaks   2 has never been/travelled
3 will nearly have finished / will have nearly finished
4 will/shall probably take / 'll probably be having
5 will certainly give   6 not usually as warm as / usually
colder than   7 suddenly slammed shut   8 doesn't
normally / normally doesn't

19.4   Verbs and idioms

1 have gone off   2 haven't come across
3 going over/through   4 put me off
5 called the race off / called off the race   6 have run
out of   7 brought him up   8 cut down on
9 fell through   10 I let you down   11 going to
bring it back   12 they fell out with

19.5   Paper 3: Use of English

41 ✓   42 up   43 and   44 a   45 ✓   46 on
47 on   48 the   49 not   50 probably   51 ✓
52 are   53 rarely   54 ✓   55 people

Thanks to ...

Charlotte Adams, who encouraged me to write this Workbook
Niki Browne, who managed the project
Maria Pylas, who edited the book, with the help of Claire Thacker
Hilary Fletcher, who researched the photos
Julie Cutter, who obtained text permissions
Ruth Carim, who checked the proofs

James Richardson, who produced the recordings
Andy Taylor, the engineer at Studio AVP
The actors who took part in the recordings

the First Certificate teachers, who read the first draft and made many helpful comments
and imaginative suggestions:

Christine Barton in Greece
Annie Broadhead in the UK
Henny Burke in Spain
Harry Crawford in France
Fiona Davis in the UK
Helena Galani in Greece
Roger Scott in the UK
Tadeusz Wolanski in Poland

and ...
Sue Gosling, who wrote the Model compositions.

Acknowledgements

The author and publishers are grateful to the following copyright holders for permission to reproduce copyright material. While every endeavour has been made, it has not been possible to identify the sources of all material used and in such cases the publishers would welcome information from copyright sources. Apologies are expressed for any omissions.

For permission to reproduce texts:

p. 7: Jonathan Watts, p. 77: Nicholas Bannister, p. 39: Paul Webster, p. 43: John Illman, p. 72: Denis Staunton, p. 87: Emily Barr, p. 97: Diane Paul all taken from articles published in *The Guardian*; *The Guardian* for p. 37 by Amelia Gentleman, p. 42: 'Katharine Viner lights a Hopi ear candle', p. 57: 'How to do well in exams', p. 59 by Michael Ellison, p. 77 by Nicholas Bannister; pp.16—17: Maurice Weaver, p. 22: Ben Fenton, p. 23 'Cheesey grins for the high rollers', pp. 82–83, pp. 92–93: Nigel Reynolds © Telegraph Group Limited 1997; pp. 27, 33: © The Economist, London; pp. 47–49: Explore Worldwide; p. 52: extract from *Real Cooking* © Nigel Slater 1997; p. 62: Cityscreen, London; p. 69: Various extracts from Cambridge English Readers.

For permission to reproduce photographs and other copyright artwork:

© Assignments/Bryn Colton for p. 57; Associated Press Photo for p. 27; Corbis SYGMA/P. Forestier for p. 39 (top); Explore Worldwide for p. 47; The Guardian/Martin Argles for p. 37; Image Bank/Elyse Lewin for p. 30 (right); Katz Pictures 1993/Richard Baker for pp. 44 (left), /Joe Pugliese/CPi 1998 for p. 89 (left); Life File/Cliff Threadgold for p. 10 (right); Network/Barry Lewis for pp. 30 (left), /J-M Charles/Rapho for p. 89 (right); The New Yorker Collection 1992 Mick Stevens from cartoonbank.com. All Rights Reserved for p. 7; The New Yorker Collection 1998 Victoria Roberts from cartoonbank.com. All Rights Reserved for p. 14; The New Yorker Collection 1987 Henry Martin from cartoonbank.com. All Rights Reserved for p. 75; Bridget Riley *White Discs 2*, 1964, Emulsion on board 41" × 39". Private Collection © 2000 Bridget Riley for p. 94; Bridget Riley *Shiver*, 1964, Emulsion on board $27\frac{1}{8}$" × $27\frac{1}{8}$". Private Collection, London © 2000 Bridget Riley for p. 95; Ross Parry Agency for p. 92; Popperfoto/Reuters for pp. 24, 84; Powerstock Zefa for p. 44 (right); Tony Stone Images/Garry Hunter for p. 77; John Walmsley for pp. 10 (left), 60.

We have been unable to trace the photographer of the picture on page 39 (bottom), and would be grateful for any information to enable us to do so.

Notes